Someone to Devour

Winning The Spiritual Battle within Human Conflict

J.T. Barksdale

PublishAmerica
Baltimore

First printing

Hardcover 978-1-4626-3373-9
Softcover 978-1-4626-3372-2
PUBLISHED BY PUBLISHAMERICA, LLLP
www.publishamerica.com
Baltimore

Printed in the United States of America

Someone to Devour

Winning The Spiritual Battle within Human Conflict

Table of Contents

Forward
7

Preface
13

Introduction
15

Chapter One
Smile in Your Face
19

Chapter Two
Modus Operandi
28

Chapter Three
Suit Up!
37

Chapter Four
The Truth, The Whole Truth, and Nothing But The Truth
42

Chapter Five
Two Wrongs Don't Make a Right
52

Chapter Six
A Peace of the Action
62

Chapter Seven
A Slap in The Faith
69

Chapter Eight
Somebody Save Me!
76

Chapter Nine
Word!
81

Chapter Ten
Do You Pray or Are You Prey?
90

Chapter Eleven
Armed and Dangerous!
94

Chapter Twelve
May I Take Your Order?
103

Conclusion
124

End Notes
131

Foreword

Jeff's life has been a journey. So has yours. Your journey and his journey are about to cross paths. Whether it is in the field of business, sports, relationships, or personal spiritual issues, one of the best things that can happen to us is to have someone who is a little further down the path let us know how to get through the maze.

Because of a specific incident in Jeff's life, he was forced to do some major reevaluation. It sent him to some serious consideration. It sent him to the Scriptures. And it sent him to some fresh conclusions. Conclusions that not only helped him, they can help you too.

In Someone to Devour you will hear the voice of someone who has traveled a pretty common journey in an uncommon way. It is pretty common to be aware of some serious personal issues. It is pretty uncommon to address them as seriously as Jeff has. You will see how the Lord led him to address them and find success through them. You will like the stories. You will laugh. You will question. You will reevaluate. You will see Scripture in a new light. You will be able to see what is ahead on your journey. And you will receive help about how to proceed.

As you read, the names of other people will come to your mind. These are people who could benefit from these stories and these truths. Just like God used Jeff in your life to help you on your journey, now you can be used in a similar way to help someone else on their journey. Don't let this book just sit on the shelf. Read it. Do it. And spread it around.

Dennis Fuqua
Author—*Living Prayer: The Lord's Prayer Alive in You*
Director—*International Renewal Ministries*

Dedication

I would like to dedicate this book to my son Adam. He is in the midst of a struggle, which I cannot even begin to fully fathom. Adam, you are an amazing young man and I know that God will use you in great ways to advance His kingdom. You have already had an incredible impact on many, pointing them to the Savior and helping them to understand God's Word within their own struggles. Although many miles separate us, rest in the truth of how much your mother and I love you and pray for you daily. As you walk with God I hope you are feeling the effect of our prayers, and you are leaning on the Lord in the low times. Your strength in the battle will always be a source of inspiration to me. With the Holy Spirit guiding your steps, I know you will be a mighty force in the battle against the devil's lies. I will always be standing in the gap for you in prayer.

All My Love,
Dad

Acknowledgments

My Beautiful Bride of 25 years—Stacy, your love and support is a true gift to me. You are an amazing model of what a Christian wife and mother should look like. Your constant love for our children; Adam, Alex, Tyler, Sydney and Madison, has impacted not only them, but all who know you. I can't imagine my life without you at my side. All My Love!

Pastor Mike & Holly Wehde—You are those rare friends that God uses in a great way. Your love, truth and wisdom have richly blessed my family and me. It has been my joy to be ministering by your side. Love You Both.

Kathy MacCloskey—I appreciate your work on this project more than I could ever express. Your input and suggestions are always welcome and have added clarity to the message within this book. Thank You So Much.

Chris Irwin—Thanks for all your creative concepts and ideas. I know your work on the cover was a gift to me, and I am so appreciative that you would lend your God given talents to this project. If anyone reading this book needs a great website designer look up Chris at www.appstronauts.com. *(You owe me one for that plug. You can buy me lunch at Thai Corner).*

Love you, brother.

Kara Fuqua—Thank you for lending your talents in photography to my book projects. I realize you didn't have a lot to work with and you still managed to make me look acceptable. We miss you guys.

Lifecoast Staff—You have been a great source of strength and growth to my family and me. Thank you for your prayers, your friendship and your leadership. We Are In The Battle Together.

Lifecoast Church—I love being a pastor at Lifecoast Church. You have encouraged, supported and prayed for the Barksdale family through some wonderful and painful times. You have been the Body of Christ to us. We could never thank you enough for all that you've done for, and with our family. We have worshipped together, learned from God's Word together, cried together and laughed together (You even laugh at my warped sense of humor). I hope there will be crowns in heaven for church members who laugh at their pastor's bad jokes. You are all a blessing.

Preface

Have you ever been in a place of darkness? Does life seem to be meaningless? If the worries of your life have become heavy and overwhelming, please take the time to read this book. I wrote it after a particularly difficult time in my own life. It wasn't sickness, or even financial trouble. Our family was struggling with heart wrenching internal circumstances, but even that wasn't the catalyst for this season of despair. I can assure you that it was a dark time, and the pressures of life were weighing heavy on me. I felt lost and adrift, not sure which direction to go. Not sure if anything I did mattered or if the people who I worked and ministered with even wanted me to continue in ministry with them.

Each of us, whether we are in ministry or work in a secular job, I'm sure have had thoughts of feeling worthless and empty at one time or another. It is from this pit that I discovered God's divine process for climbing from the depths of despair to a renewed sense of purpose and fulfillment. Since the occurrence of those events, I have felt compelled to share that process in the pages of this book. As you read, I hope you can feel the presence of the Holy Spirit come into your world and lift you from your darkness as He lifted me from mine. Whatever circumstances you find yourself in, if you are hurting, I pray for you to be blessed, not by my words, but by the truth of God's Word, the source of my restoration.

Introduction

The world we live in is often difficult to understand. We live each day trying to do our best to make a living, raise our families, affect our communities for good, at the same time trying to keep our journey as trouble free as possible. Unfortunately, much to our dismay, trouble inevitably discovers a way to find us. Whether financial, relational, physical or occupational, Trouble finds his way into our lives and brings his extended family with him. Trouble's family members are anger, bitterness, revenge, spite, depression, emptiness and self-pity. Have you met the family? Perhaps you have only met a few of them. If they are not dealt with quickly and directly Trouble's family will continue to arrive. The members of this family aren't shy and non-assuming at all. Once they meet you they like to move right in, unpack their bags, and make themselves right at home. They can turn a peaceful and joy-filled life into daily feelings of heartache, anguish and discord. Once these feelings have fully moved into your heart, their dirty laundry will often be a myopic pursuit of "one-upmanship." One-upmanship is the practice of attempting to outdo or show yourself to be superior to a rival or opponent.

I have come to discover that this negative line of thinking, in many cases may not even originate within our own thoughts. It has been my experience that many of these thoughts originate from the spiritual world.

What does all that mean? It means there is a battle going on in the mind and the souls of every human being on this planet. The fighting began thousands of years ago when Adam and Eve walked in the Garden located in Eden. Adam and Eve had their thinking influenced by an outside source. On that day Satan fired the first shot in a spiritual war that continues to this day. Even though it is a spiritual battle, taking place in the unseen world, it has real and often devastating implications in the physical world in which we live. This battle impacts anything from minor conflicts between neighbors, friends and even church members to wars being fought between countries. It doesn't matter if the conflict is small or large, between two people or between two nations; the reality is that these conflicts can be physically and emotionally devastating to all involved. But beyond what we can see and feel, an even greater battle is being fought in the spiritual arena. For those who are not aware of the existence of the spiritual world, this information might seem like a mere ghost story given to scare people into thinking "religiously." But to those who have witnessed or have been influenced by the battle of which I am speaking, to them, it is all too real.

As a pastor, I gave a message on this topic after a tumultuous time battling the enemy. It was through this battle that I discovered the process I will share throughout this book. This is not a new or hidden process; the Bible has always had this information within its pages. I have simply been led, through great need to search this information out and to place it into a workable process. I then discovered the implementation of this process yielded amazing and life transforming results. In the weeks and months that followed I realized that if I, as a long time Christian, had to hunt through scripture for the verses and truths that I desperately hungered for in my hour of uncertainty, people in general might need a little assistance in discovering what God led me to after a week of fasting and praying for answers. Believe me when I tell you I am nothing special. Maybe that's why it took me a week to find the truths in these scriptures that I had known "about" for many, many years. Perhaps as you continue to read you will understand why I say, "This is nothing new." However, even if you say to yourself, as I did, "I already know all of these verses" it is my hope and prayer that the process and perspective that God led me through can be the road that leads you or someone you love, to the peace and forgiveness that I was given. My prayer is that this book will give people and churches in conflict a tangible process by which they can extend and receive the forgiveness that leads to reconciliation.

Chapter One

Smile in Your Face
(Do I have something between my teeth?)

Before I became a pastor I worked for twenty-six years as a Correction Officer in the prison system of Massachusetts. If you read my last book (All Good People Go to Heaven?)[1], you already know I often use my prison experiences from those years as analogies and backdrops to illustrate the points I am trying to make in each chapter. You also may be aware that I have just given a shameless plug for my first book. Sorry, I couldn't resist!

For those who are not familiar with the set up of a prison, a cellblock is the area where many inmate-housing cells are located. A cellblock can contain anywhere from 24 to 100 cells and usually one Correction Officer runs each block. This Officer is often referred to as the block-officer.

Working as a block-officer, on a routine day at the prison, a fight between two inmates had broken out in another cellblock. I locked my block and responded to the emergency only to witness that the inmates had already been separated, hand-cuffed and were being escorted to Lock-up. The medical staff tended to their minor wounds and they were placed into neighboring cells within the Lock-up unit.

After several days in Lock-up, the two inmates were released. As they returned to the general population, something strange began to take place. What transpired was so unusual it became obvious to all of us who worked there, and was a topic of several roll call and lunch room conversations. These two inmates, who had never liked each other before the fight, began to spend a lot of time together. They were seen in the gym and working out together. They were seen sitting together at every meal in the chow hall. They were constantly hanging out together in the inmate yard. They were, seemingly, inseparable.

That was not the only difference in there relationship. It was apparent that while the two of them were getting closer as friends, all of their previous companions were being shut out of this "exclusive" relationship. These unlikely companions continued this relationship for many months. I say unlikely companions because one of the inmates was a short white man of Irish descent, while the other was a tall black man of Puerto Rican descent. In a normal community this is certainly not strange, but in a prison setting, this is just not a normal pairing.

As I said, these two continued to be seen together almost exclusively for months. One morning, many months later, as I arrived at work, I was informed that there had been a stabbing the night before. The altercation was between the two inmates you have just read about. The shorter inmate had stabbed the taller one. The shank had been thrust into his chest three times, just under his heart. There was no doubt about the assailant. The stabbing took place in the main corridor just outside the gym. Although it was around a corner, just outside of the view of the corridor cameras, several inmate witnesses had observed the stabbing, not to mention that the victim himself was all too aware of who had attacked him, and relayed that information to the medical staff before losing consciousness.

As the Property Sergeant, I was instructed to assist the IPS (Inner Perimeter Security) team with inventorying and storing the property which they had just removed from the cell of the inmate assailant, which now, of course, was a crime scene. As I arrived on the scene the Sergeant in charge of the investigation showed me a note that had been taped to the stainless steal mirror which was bolted to the wall of the inmate's cell. After reading the note all I could do was look at the Sergeant with obvious shock on my face

The Note:

If you want to kill your enemy, become his friend. Not for a day, not for a week, not even for a month, but for a year. Then you can stab him in the heart as he smiles in your face.

It's very hard for most people to comprehend this kind of hatred. Hatred so deep and passionate it will even write down words to further inspire it's evil actions. Hatred that plots, schemes and plans harm toward the object of the hate. As I recalled this event from my past, I am truly convinced that this is a physical world example of a spiritual world reality. This is the model of hatred that Satan has for every person that has ever walked on this earth. He hates us with a passion that transcends time and space. It is that hatred we spoke of which began thousands of years ago, and it will not die until Satan is given his final punishment.

Most people have certainly heard of Satan. He is known by many names; The Devil, Beelzebub, The Serpent and The Father of Lies just to name a few. Whether or not you are aware of his names and titles is not the most important thing. But there are three things we all need to understand about Satan; 1) We need to understand who he really is. 2) We need to understand what he is planning. 3) Most importantly, we must understand how he can influence our thoughts and actions.

In order to gain a better understanding of this evil entity, it will be necessary for us to use the Bible. It is the only record we have for the events leading up to Satan's fall from perfection. If we can get a better understanding of who or what Satan is, we will be better able to understand his plan of action. When we understand his plan, we can then take a purposeful approach to defend ourselves against him.

The Birth of Evil

Satan is identified in Scripture as an angel. All angels were created within the event of Heaven's creation. Although there is no specific record of angels being created, the Bible does denote that Jesus created all things and clearly records that the "things in heaven" were created by Him.

Genesis 1:1

In the beginning God created the heavens and the earth.

Colossians 1:16

For by him [Jesus] all things were created: things in heaven and on earth, visible and invisible, whether thrones or powers or rulers or authorities; all things were created by him and for him.

Since the Bible mentions angels hundreds of times, we must conclude that angels exist and they were created when the heavens were created. By cross referencing the Genesis passage with the Colossians passage, we can see that angels were created within the general time frame of "In the beginning…" They were created when "The Heavens" were created. They were created before Adam and Eve, which took place five days later, on the sixth day of the creation week (Genesis 1:26-31).

The term angel is an anglicized word from the Greek term (angelos). The word translates literally as "messenger." Angel is a general term describing these spiritual beings. Within Scripture we find many other terms used to describe more specific types, categories, and rankings of angels. Some of these terms are: Thrones, Powers, Rulers and Authorities (Colossians 1:16), Cherubim (Genesis 3:24), Seraphs (Isaiah 6:2), Princes (Daniel 10:13) and of course Archangels (Jude 9). I mention these rankings of angels so that we can be aware of the diversity of the angelic realm as well as the frequency of their appearance within Scripture. The Bible does speak often about angels and their appearances, which lead us to conclude that there is a spiritual realm that is unseen. What we seldom consider is that this unseen world is even more vast and creative than the physical world we see and live in.

Satan's early days are described in the Old Testament book of Ezekiel chapter twenty-eight. Ezekiel was a prophet of God who wrote as the Holy Spirit led him.

Ezekiel 28:1-2

The word of the LORD came to me: [2] "Son of man, say to the ruler of Tyre, 'This is what the Sovereign LORD says:

Ezekiel is told to address this writing to the ruler of Tyre. The chapter goes on to describe an egotistical ruler of an ancient city (Tyre). As the Word of the Lord continues through the prophet Ezekiel, it becomes evident that the words are no longer describing a mere man, but have begun a description of Satan and his beginning.

Ezekiel 28:12-17

This is what the Sovereign LORD says: "'You were the model of perfection, full of wisdom and perfect in beauty. [13] *You were in Eden, the garden of God; every precious stone adorned you: ruby, topaz and emerald, chrysolite, onyx and jasper, sapphire, turquoise and beryl. Your settings and mountings were made of gold; on the day you were created they were prepared.* [14] *You were anointed as a guardian cherub, for so I ordained you. You were on the holy mount of God; you walked among the fiery stones.* [15] *You were blameless in your ways from the day you were created till wickedness was found in you.* [16] *...and you sinned. So I drove you in disgrace from the mount of God, and I expelled you, O guardian cherub, from among the fiery stones.* [17] *Your heart became proud on account of your beauty, and you corrupted your wisdom because of your splendor.*

Whether the ruler of Tyre is possessed by Satan or just greatly influenced by him is unclear, but it is clear that God is giving us a peek at what Satan was like before his fall, and also what was the cause of his sin and the birth of evil.

Satan is the most beautiful as well as the wisest angel that has ever been created. He was created in the order of Cherubs, which are guardian angels. Satan was given the position of guardian over God's creation. He was large and in charge! There was nothing within creation that could even come close to competing with him. After creating the heaven and the earth, God went on to create animals, birds, reptiles, insects and then man. This was the day that changed Satan forever.

Genesis 1:27-28

So God created man in his own image, in the image of God he created him; male and female he created them. [28] *God blessed them and said to them, "Be fruitful and increase in number; fill the earth and subdue it.*

The word translated "subdue" is from the Hebrew term (kahvahsh) which literally means to bring into submission or dominate. I can imagine Satan questioning God's Words, "What did God just say? '...increase in number, fill the earth and dominate it?' That can't be right; God gave the earth to me! How can He now give dominion of the earth to these mere mortals?" In Satan's mind he could have done things so much better. Satan was so impressed with his own beauty and wisdom that he believed, and still does believe, he can undermine God's plan and bring all things under his own rule.

What Satan missed, or just simply disagreed with, is that he was given SPIRITUAL dominion over the earth, and Adam and Eve (The Mere Mortals) were given PHYSICAL dominion over the earth. Nothing has changed! God didn't renege on His word. In fact, on at least two occasions, Jesus reaffirmed that Satan is "the prince (ruler) of this world" (John 12:31; John 16:11). In Ephesians 2:2 Satan is identified as "the ruler of the kingdom of the air." The Greek word translated as "air" is (pneumatos). This is where we get our English word pneumatic, meaning "air-driven." This very same Greek word is often translated in Scripture as the word 'spirit'. Satan continues to rule in the spiritual realm of this world, a world we cannot see. Even though our physical eyes cannot see into the spiritual realm, we are still greatly affected by the actions of Satan and those many angels who followed him (Revelation 12:4) on his quest of hate against God and the object of God's affections; people.

That is where we are on our journey of life. The object of one who hates us enough to plot, plan and scheme in order to draw us away from God and toward destruction. The struggle is real, the struggle is relentless and, even worse, the struggle is unseen.

Ephesians 6:12

For our struggle is not against flesh and blood, but against the rulers, against the authorities, against the powers of this dark world and against the spiritual forces of evil in the heavenly realms.

If you are going through life alone and with no plan of defense, you are leaving yourself open for attack. Satan wants to lure you into feeling safe and secure with him by leading you to people that are enemies of God. He wants you to be isolated from those that are close to God because Satan knows that they will reveal him for who he is. He is becoming your friend so he can "stab you in the heart as you smile in his face." Most people go through life totally unaware that they are even in a battle and are being led toward destruction.

If you have read this far, then you are one step closer to mounting a defense against the one who wants only to destroy you. Some of you are reading and thinking, since you are already a Christian, this doesn't apply to you. Well, you couldn't be more wrong! It applies to Christians just as much, if not more than to those who have not asked for forgiveness and trusted Jesus as their Lord and Savior. Believers are on the front lines of the battle. For those who have trusted Jesus as Savior, Satan cannot change your eternal destination, but what he can do is slow, redirect and, if possible, stop your impact on those who know nothing about God. Sadly, these same people know even less about Satan and the spiritual struggle they are in. If you decide to read on, and I hope and pray you do, I would ask you to take the time to look up each verse referenced and mark it in your own Bible so that you will always have your God given weapons of defense at your disposal.

Chapter Two

Modus Operandi (The Modus The Merrier)

When I was a young man I played a lot of baseball and fast pitch softball. It was a great way to relieve the tensions of the very high risk and high stress job of working in the prison. It seemed during my career, the more stressful my job became, the more softball I would play. It was not uncommon for me to go away and play in a weekend long tournament with games being played from Friday night until Sunday afternoon. I know that some of you were hoping for another prison story, but this event in my life reveals the truth better than any prison story I could recall. So perhaps in an extended way, this is a "prison life" story!

On one of those softball weekends I was playing with a team in a state championship qualifying tournament. We were playing against other teams from all over the state who were also trying to qualify for the state championship. During our final game of the weekend, we fell behind early and had to chip away at a big deficit while trying to hold the other team from scoring any more runs. Well, our plan seemed to be working as we came within one run, with just one inning left to play.

Unfortunately, the other team scored a run in the top of the final inning and we were heading into our last at bat down by two runs. We did get our first batter on base but then the next two hitters quickly made outs. The next batter got a single and that was followed with a walk, setting up the scenario that every kid dreams about when we played pick-up games in our back yards! Bases loaded, two outs, bottom of the ninth in the championship game. This was only a state qualifier—but you get the picture. I walked to the batters box from the on deck circle trying to solidify a plan of attack. First of all, I did not want to make the last out of the game! That much I knew for sure. Secondly, I had not done well against this pitcher. I had gotten one hit in four at bats, but my hit had only been a Texas Leaguer (a weak pop up that lands where no one can reach it). The pitcher we had been facing had an extremely good change up that he had used successfully against me all four of my previous at bats.

For those of you who are not familiar with a "change up," it is a pitch in which a pitcher uses his normal throwing motion but throws the ball much, much slower than his normal fastball or even his curveball. This pitcher had me off balance with this pitch all day. I knew it, and he knew it! If I had any hope of getting a hit I needed to lay off the change up, and look for his fastball, which also was very good. In my mind I told myself over and over again, "Change up—no, fast ball—swing." I began to walk toward the batters box, stopped briefly to pray for focus, and proceeded to walk to home plate. The first pitch was a fastball inside, which caused me to back away from home plate. "Ball one!" Said the umpire. I was anticipating a change up next and just as I expected, the next pitch was a change up over the outside corner. I watched it go by. "Strike one!" was the call from the Umpire. The count is now One Ball and One Strike. I anticipated another change up, and sure enough, the pitcher threw me another change up, but it was high and out of the strike zone. With the count two balls and one strike, I now had the advantage. The odds the pitcher would not throw a third change up were very low as this would allow me to see the same pitch three times in a row. The pitcher would not want to risk the count going to a three balls and one strike count with the bases loaded. The odds were very high for the pitcher to throw his best and most accurate pitch, a fast ball. I backed out of the batter's box, took a deep breath, prayed again for composure, and stepped back in, focusing all my concentration on hitting a fastball over on the outside corner of the plate. The pitcher wound up and the pitch was delivered—a fastball on the outside corner. I hit a line drive that went off the fence in right-center field. All three base runners scored and we won the game!

Why do I tell this story? Not to pat myself on the back or reminisce about glory days, but to demonstrate, through a real life experience, how much easier it is to react correctly if you know what the enemy is going to throw at you. I had watched the pitcher, noted what he had done in the past, and also noted that what he had done had been successful in getting me out or minimizing my effectiveness. My plan was based on knowing his strengths and my weaknesses. My success was only possible because I knew what he was going to throw.

We can take this same advantage when battling Satan. He has not changed his plan of attack since the game began. He knows what works on mankind, and he keeps using it. For Satan, the old saying rings true again and again, "If it ain't broke—don't fix it." God has revealed Satan's plan of attack in His Word. It has been given to us so that we can recognize it, prepare for it, and react to it successfully. Here is the plan in a single sentence.

1 John 2:16

For everything in the world—the cravings of sinful man, the lust of his eyes and the boasting of what he has and does—comes not from the Father but from the world.

Within this verse are the three areas where Satan will exploit our weaknesses. Most people are not aware that they are vulnerable in one, or in all of these areas. The first area of weakness is; the cravings of sinful man. Since we all are descendants of Adam, we all have within us the curse of original sin. The Bible tells us that sin and death entered the world through one man, and that man was Adam.

Romans 5:12

Therefore, just as sin entered the world through one man, and death through sin, and in this way death came to all men, because all sinned—

This sin nature, this craving toward selfishness is something that is in every person. Whenever we do not have our spiritual guard up, whenever we get comfortable with where we are in our relationship with God, we default to self-centeredness. It is who we are. We need to come to the realization that we all have this weakness in our character. Only then can we begin to use this weakness to our advantage. I will have more on that in the chapters to come. For now, we just need to focus on Satan's battle plan and the first area of his attack is our sinful cravings.

The second area of weakness is the lust of our eyes. We are always trying to look at the things that will tempt our mind to places it should not go. It can be different temptations for everyone, but the root weakness is the same. We can't help looking at that girl, that guy, that car, that food, and the list goes on and on. It has been said that the eyes are the window to the soul. Satan knows that he can get instant access to our mind if he just throws something physically attractive in front of us. Billboards! Magazine ads! Television commercials! I'm sure you will agree Satan has laid the groundwork for an unrelenting onslaught on the eyes. Are you beginning to see the truth of what has been written?

Lastly, the final area of weakness is the boasting of what we have or what we can do. This one is an attack on the very blessings from God. If we know and believe that God is who He says He is, then everything we have and everything we are capable of doing is a direct gift and blessing from God. But Satan wants to use the very things that God gives us and in turn, use them as a tool for selfish thinking and move us further and further from our relationship with God.

These tactics that God has revealed to us in 1 John, one of the last books of the Bible to be written, were used in the Garden of Eden to tempt Eve in the first book of the Bible.

Genesis 3:4-6

...the serpent said to the woman. 5 *"For God knows that when you eat of it your eyes will be opened, and you will be like God, knowing good and evil."* 6 *When the woman saw that the fruit of the tree was good for food and pleasing to the eye, and also desirable for gaining wisdom, she took some and ate it. She also gave some to her husband, who was with her, and he ate it.*

This portion of Scripture shows us clearly that Satan's evil plan was put into effect right from the beginning. The three areas of his game plan are easily seen from both his words and Eve's response. Temptation Part One: The Cravings of sinful man—"*When the woman saw that the fruit of the tree was good for food...*" Hunger is an amazingly powerful motivator. Even though there were plenty of other fruit trees in the Garden, Eve obviously had her thoughts set on how satisfying that particular fruit might taste. Temptation Part Two: The Lust of the eyes—"*When the woman saw that the fruit of the tree was good for food and pleasing to the eye, ...*" Not only would it satisfy her hunger with great taste, it was a delight to her eye. This was a great looking fruit! It was probably the most appealing piece of fruit in the entire garden. She wouldn't just be stuck eating a lame old apple or peach! She would eat the amazing fruit from the tree of the knowledge of good and evil. And finally Temptation Part Three: The Boasting of what we have or what we can do—"*and also desirable for gaining wisdom, ...*" She would know good and evil like God. They (Adam and Eve) would be elevated to the same level as God. At least that is what Satan led them to believe.

We all know the rest of the story, Eve gave some to her husband, who was with her, and they both ate of the fruit. Satan had won his first battle which only solidified that the evil plan he had devised for destroying mankind had been successfully tested. He was ready to use this simple but effective tactic through tens of thousands of angels, who followed him in his war against God and all of creation.

This is Satan's modus operandi. His method of operation. This particular plan was so solidified in the playbook of Satan that he used this same tactic when he brought temptation upon Jesus after He had fasted for forty days in the desert.

Matthew 4:1-11

Then Jesus was led by the Spirit into the desert to be tempted by the devil. 2 *After fasting forty days and forty nights, he was hungry.* [3] *The tempter came to him and said, "If you are the Son of God, tell these stones to become bread."* [4] *Jesus answered, "It is written: 'Man does not live on bread alone, but on every word that comes from the mouth of God.'"* [5] *Then the devil took him to the holy city and had him stand on the highest point of the temple.* [6] *"If you are the Son of God," he said, "throw yourself down. For it is written: "'He will command his angels concerning you, and they will lift you up in their hands, so that you will not strike your foot against a stone.'"* [7] *Jesus answered him, "It is also written: 'Do not put the Lord your God to the test.'"* [8] *Again, the devil took him to a very high mountain and showed him all the kingdoms of the world and their splendor.* [9] *"All this I will give you," he said, "if you will bow down and worship me."* [10] *Jesus said to him, "Away from me, Satan! For it is written: 'Worship the Lord your God, and serve him only.'"* [11] *Then the devil left him, and angels came and attended him.*

When we know the battle plan, it is easy to see. Satan said to Jesus in the third verse, *"tell these stones to become bread."* As Jesus was hungry from fasting, Satan was counting on Jesus' cravings for food to be the controlling factor in His decision making. He then tempted Jesus with these words, *"If you are the Son of God," he said, "throw yourself down. For it is written: "'He will command his angels concerning you, and they will lift you up in their hands, so that you will not strike your foot against a stone."* Satan thought he would be tricky by changing the order. He actually expected Jesus to show off what He had, or was able to do. That's how confident Satan is in this plan he has crafted. He continued with his final temptation as he tried to get Jesus to lust with His eyes, *"...Again, the devil took him to a very high mountain and showed him all the kingdoms of the world and their splendor."* We cannot think so highly of ourselves that we fall into the lie that Satan will not try these same tactics on us. If Satan tried to tempt Jesus Christ, God in flesh, you and I are mere sheep among wolves when it comes to Satan's view of our ability to resist him and his army.

There are some who go through life never knowing the first thing about spiritual warfare. Then there are others who seem to have knowledge of the battle that is raging around them but for some reason believe that they are Switzerland or something (Switzerland remained neutral during WWII)[2]. If they never acknowledge its existence they won't be affected or influenced by it. Let me be clear. I am not suggesting that we start looking for demons under every rock. But to ignore the existence of Satan and his minions is just as dangerous as over focusing on them. The principle of keeping our focus on Christ should never be placed on the sidelines to go chase Satan.

Hebrews 12:2

Let us fix our eyes on Jesus, the author and perfecter of our faith,...

The truth is that the more we fix our eyes on Jesus, the more Satan will try to distract our focus. He will use the tactics I have described in this chapter. We cannot allow the devil to use our selfishness as a weapon against us. We must learn to be self-controlled.

1 Peter 5:8

Be self-controlled and alert. Your enemy the devil prowls around like a roaring lion looking for someone to devour.

It is eternally important for us to realize that human conflict is, at its root, a spiritual battle. When others do not do or say the things that we, in our selfishness, believe they should say or do, we get offended and respond negatively. If we fail to understand this foundational truth, we leave ourselves open for unresolved conflict and the "Trouble" that comes with it.

Chapter Three

Suit Up!
(The Red Suit not a Lawsuit)

In the prisons I worked in there were many occasions when an inmate would become violent and uncooperative. Many times these inmates would arm themselves with homemade weapons. These inmates could be in a cell or out in the open threatening anyone and everyone who came near. It was at this point that an Extraction Team would be assembled for the purposes of isolating, disarming and removing the uncooperative inmate and relocate him to a secure cell in the lock-up unit. These teams were authorized to use whatever force was reasonably necessary to accomplish this mission. Every officer is trained for being part of an Extraction Team. During this training we learn about all the protective gear we will be wearing and the proper way to put it on. The gear consists of a helmet with face shield, a stab proof vest, elbow pads, knee pads, shin guards, slash guards for the forearms and sap-gloves (gloves with a protective hard leather backhand). The final piece of equipment was a large concave plexi-glass shield, which the lead man on the team would use to protect the team. The shield was also a very effective tool for directing and controlling the inmate. After learning about all the equipment and the proper way to wear it, we then executed full contact extractions with Correction Officer's volunteering to pose as inmates (also dressed in full protective gear). If the training had only consisted of how to wear the gear, we would have had to figure out for ourselves how to effectively use the armor to our best advantage. It was putting the plan and knowledge into action that allowed us to be effective Extraction Team members. As a young man, this full contact training was extremely exhilarating! I enjoyed both training with the teams as well as volunteering to be the inmate. It was this real contact training as well as the dozens of inmate extractions over the course of my career that both engrained the process in my mind, and built the confidence needed to be an effective Extraction Team member.

The same is true of the spiritual battle. A person can receive all the protective armor in the world, but if he is never shown how to use it, and if he never actually gets into any real action, it won't be very effective in protecting him.

The Word of God tells us of the armor we can use to defeat the spiritual attacks of the evil one. But few people that I know have a firm grasp of exactly how to use the gear effectively in daily combat with the enemy.

Ephesians 6:12-17

For our struggle is not against flesh and blood, but against the rulers, against the authorities, against the powers of this dark world and against the spiritual forces of evil in the heavenly realms. 13 Therefore put on the full armor of God, so that when the day of evil comes, you may be able to stand your ground, and after you have done everything, to stand. 14 Stand firm then, with the belt of truth buckled around your waist, with the breastplate of righteousness in place, 15 and with your feet

fitted with the readiness that comes from the gospel of peace.
[16] *In addition to all this, take up the shield of faith, with which you can extinguish all the flaming arrows of the evil one.* [17] *Take the helmet of salvation and the sword of the Spirit, which is the word of God.*

The weapons which are matched with metaphorical pieces of armor are revealed to us in these verses. I have heard many pastors and teachers speak on this portion of Scripture but on every occasion I have been left with concepts and action steps that have little or no connection to the real world that people live in. The attack I mentioned earlier gave me opportunity to not only search for weapons to use against the enemy, but also to pray for God to show me how to use them effectively. The actual weapons without their armor metaphors are as follows; Truth, Righteousness, Peace (The Gospel of Peace), Faith, Salvation and The Word of God.

These are the weapons that we must use against our enemy the devil. Though these are listed as armor and can be used in unison, I have found them to be far more effective as a set of steps to both defend against attacks and avoid attacks altogether. These steps are equally effective for the person who is seeking God for the first time, as well as the person who has already received Christ as Savior and Lord. When we strip away the metaphorical armor, a step-by-step process reveals itself that can both lead someone to a relationship with the Savior or defend the believer against the devil's attacks. Don't misunderstand me, the armor is an important part of the overall truth of this portion of Scripture, and we will cover that later.

Ephesians 6:12-17 As a Salvation Plan

If you are seeking a relationship with God for the first time, Ephesians 6:12-17 becomes a Salvation Plan. The first step in your salvation plan is Truth. If you are seeking to discover God, the Creator of all things, you are searching for Truth, perhaps for the first time in your life. There is a God who created you and loves you. He desires for you to know Him in a personal way. Once you have come to believe this as truth, it will change your perspective on every aspect of life. But for now, continue on to the next step, which is Righteousness. I know that Righteousness sounds like an archaic word that has no real meaning today. Righteousness actually does have a deep theological meaning to it. We will cover this in more detail in a later chapter. But it also has a secondary meaning, which I believe applies to those who have newly discovered truth. To them righteousness means to start doing things God's way. So what is God's way? In order to discover God's way for you to have a relationship with Him, you will need to open a Bible and read what God has written to you. Beginning your steps toward righteousness (doing things God's way), for right now, is moving to the next step—Peace. The actual verse says "The Gospel of Peace." This peace is not peace as in the absence of war. It is Peace with God. The Gospel, (Gospel literally translates as Good News) the good news of the Bible is the only thing that will bring you into a position of Peace with God. The Gospel is coming to a place in your heart where you realize that you have offended God by not acknowledging Him in your words, actions and beliefs. The Bible calls these offenses "sin." You have come to a place where you are willing to recognize your sin and ask God for forgiveness. God sent His Son Jesus to pay the penalty for our sin. Jesus' death, burial and resurrection paid our debt in full. This is where each step begins to roll right into the next. When you ask God for His forgiveness through Jesus the Son, you are taking a step of Faith. You believe that His forgiveness is yours. It is at that point you have received Salvation, which is the next step. Lastly, but certainly not least, is The Word of God. This is the step that will send you back through the chain for a deeper and stronger set of weapons, which will be needed now that you are a soldier in the Army of The Lord.

We have merely gone through the first layer of these weapons. The first layer as you have seen, is for the person who is seeking God for the first time. But for those of us who have known Jesus as Savior for any length of time, we are all too aware of how relentless and scheming Satan can be toward The Body of Christ (The Church). If you want to discover some amazingly effective weapons that you can take hold of, and begin to train and use in your struggle against our common enemy, please keep reading as I share the process I prayerfully discovered. As you read on I will be sharing this process in painful, but sometimes humorous detail. I want everyone to discover, through God's Word, these weapons which He has always intended for us to have at our disposal.

Chapter Four

The Truth, The Whole Truth and Nothing But The Truth (The Elusive Trinity)

When someone takes the stand in a court of law they are required to raise their right hand and swear an oath, "Do you swear to tell the truth, the whole truth and nothing but the truth?" As a Corrections Officer I have been to court on many occasions as a witness or plaintiff in cases against inmates. But it was a traffic court testimony that revealed a deeper meaning of this word "truth" and what it means within the oath that I had sworn. While driving home from the prison one day, a police car with its siren and emergency lights on came up behind me as I approached an intersection with traffic signals. I did what is required by law when an emergency vehicle approaches. I slowed, moved to the right and let the vehicle pass. As I said, I was already nearing the intersection and the police car slowed as soon as it passed me because the light at the intersection was red. As the police car edged into the intersection, from my vantage point, I could see a vehicle approaching the intersection from the left at normal driving speed. I looked right at the driver to see if he saw the police car entering the intersection. The driver looked up briefly to see the traffic light, which for him was green. The driver then looked down again toward the center dash area within his vehicle. The vehicle approaching from the left continued into the intersection without slowing, crashing into the left rear fender of the police car. The impact sent the police car spinning around multiple times, finally coming to an abrupt stop when it hit the curb and light pole on the far, right side of the intersection. I pulled off the road, got out of my car in order to assist both drivers. I later gave my statement to the police officers that had responded to the scene of the accident.

Several months later I received a phone call from an attorney who was representing the person who was driving the vehicle which had struck the police car. This attorney asked me a few questions about my eye witness report, which I answered. He then asked me if I would be willing to testify in court. I asked the attorney if he was sure it was me he needed for his case and he assured me that my testimony was important. I agreed to be at court on the appointed day and time to give testimony to what I had observed.

The day arrived for the hearing and both lawyers were present, as well as the drivers of both vehicles. The attorney who had contacted me as to the questions I would be asked briefed me. His questions were in regard to the color of the traffic signals. Did the police car have a red light? Did the police car enter into the intersection while the light was still red? After that meeting the attorney for the police officer approached me in regard to my testimony. She asked me some questions about a totally different portion of my written report. She informed me that I would be the first witness called to take the stand. I was a little confused as it seemed that I was an important witness for both cases.

The police officer's attorney called me to the stand. I swore my oath to tell the truth, the whole truth and nothing but the truth and then she asked me to describe what I had seen. I described the events as I described them in my report. The other driver's attorney interrupted only once to object to a speculation I had made as to what the driver may have been looking at on the dash board. I had made an assumption that to me it looked like he was adjusting the radio. The objection was sustained, and I continued. At the completion of my testimony the attorney who had initially contacted me, stood up with a perplexed look on his face and proceeded to ask me some questions. His first question was, "You say you could see the face of the driver as he approached the intersection?" I replied, "Yes—that's true." He then asked, "Isn't there, in fact, a small grove of pine trees off the road to the left at that intersection?" "Yes, there is." I replied. He then asked, "How then, could you see the face of the driver if the pine trees were between him and you?" My reply seemed to really upset him. I simply said, "Since I was able to see his face as he approached the intersection, apparently the pine trees were not in the way." The attorney then shouted his next question, "Do you realize that you were summoned here by my office?" Surprised by his anger, I looked at the judge, who was awaiting my response, I turned and looked back to the attorney, I answered his question but also asked a question of my own, "Yes sir, I am aware of that. Does that change the truth?" The attorney waved his arms and exclaimed, "No further questions." The other attorney said, "I have no further questions for this witness." The judge told me I was dismissed. As I looked at the judge before stepping down from the witness stand, he smiled and nodded at me.

It was this event in my life that made me realize that truth is often not what we expect it to be. That attorney had seen my report; he had even spoken to me on two occasions. I never changed or added anything to my story. Even my assumption about the radio was in my original police report. Because he summonsed me, I can only surmise that he thought I would only testify about carefully selected truths from the event. Truths like; the police car had a red light; or that his client had a green light. Both of these statements are true. But the whole truth was the determining factor in who was at fault in this accident. The judge ruled the driver of the civilian vehicle was at fault. I later learned that although he listened to the testimony of all the witnesses, my testimony was the deciding factor in the case. The whole truth.

When Satan attacks us, his initial assault is aimed at truth. He hates truth because it is in its absence that he thrives. Jesus was so clear when He revealed this area of Satan's character.

John 8:44

He (the devil) was a murderer from the beginning, not holding to the truth, for there is no truth in him. When he lies, he speaks his native language, for he is a liar and the father of lies.

For the child of God Ephesians 6:12-17 easily converts from a Salvation Plan to a Battle Plan. The very first step God lists in this Battle Plan is Truth. This is no accident. Truth is often the first area of attack. As we identify this important first step it is vital that we know what to look for. Truth isn't always as obvious as it may appear. Just because we believe it to be true doesn't necessarily mean it actually is true.

The First Step in The Battle Plan

If you are in a place of darkness, confusion or uncertainty, it is absolutely essential that you begin by separating the truth from the lies. In my circumstances, this step required a time of fasting and prayer. I am not saying this is what everyone needs to do, but you will need to do whatever it takes to get yourself to a place where you can perform an honest self-examination, as well as an unbiased assessment of the circumstances which led you to your current situation, or state of mind. You may need to invite the input of a trusted friend. This friend must be honest and bold enough to give you information that you may not be in a position to see, in and of yourself. These friends are few and far between. But they are characterized by wanting to see the best in you, and those around you. They are not trying to even a score or take sides against you or with you.

Discovering and embracing Truth is the first and most important step in the Battle Plan. Because it is the foundation for the remaining steps, it is also the most difficult. Satan will infiltrate this process with a bombardment of lies and misdirection. He wants you nowhere near the truth because he is fully aware that truth and lies cannot occupy the same space.

To help you understand how I arrived at each step of this process, I will attempt to explain my feelings, thoughts and actions or (non actions) as a conduit for you to compare your own feelings and circumstances against.

This journey began when some things had been revealed to me about myself. I was already aware of some uneasiness and tension within our ministry team but I was unaware that I was the underlying cause of the discomfort. Those rare friends I mentioned earlier were the catalyst that sent me down this path of discovery. I asked them if they knew what the cause of the tension was. With fear and trembling, they shared with me the reality of the situation. My words, actions and mannerisms had greatly impacted several close friends and coworkers in ministry in a very negative way. I was the cause of the tension! At first,

I became defensive and pointed fingers in every direction. I like to describe my response this way; I lied, cried, denied and justified! After the initial "Shock and Awe" bombardment had subsided, the knowledge I had gained left me in a very dark place, feeling down and defeated. I was unsure of myself, feeling unnecessary, unappreciated and totally lost as to what to do next. My first thoughts were in the areas of blaming, leaving, retaliating, and all the sarcastic and hurtful comebacks that my mind could process. And for those who know me well, I can be fairly quick witted and sarcastic! If you throw me a straight line I can bring the punch line with gusto! I was focused only on me, and the one-upmanship I spoke of earlier. It was from this pity-pit that I finally began to seek God for direction.

As I sat alone pondering every possible negative thing to say to those who had hurt me, my heart began to realize that I needed to bring these thoughts to God before they got totally out of my control. That's when I finally heard from God. After pondering a particularly hurtful and cutting remark, this is what I heard, "That was a really good come back Jeff—but you can never say that to anyone. That one is just for you and me to hear." God entered into my anguish and actually made me smile! It was at that point I knew He was going to work this out. I still didn't know how long the process would take. But I knew as long as I kept returning to the Truth, He would never let me down. It should come as no surprise that as we embrace truth, God reveals Himself. But so often we forget the fact that Jesus told us that He is truth.

John 14:6

Jesus answered, "I am the way and the truth and the life. No one comes to the Father except through me.

As I fasted and prayed, I asked God to reveal to me what I needed to know. The first verse He brought me to was this.

Romans 12:3

Do not think of yourself more highly than you ought, but rather think of yourself with sober judgment, in accordance with the measure of faith God has given you.

God was beginning to show me the Battle Plan that would lead me out of that dark place. The way up is down. We need to stop trying to justify what's been done. Instead, take a sober, objective look at ourselves. Because the reality is the only thing each of us can change—is us. We can do all the finger pointing we want, and we might even be right, but until others look at themselves they will not change either. Do you truly want to be all God wants you to be as you face your current struggle or the struggles to come? Then begin to weigh who you are, and what you do, against truth.

I must warn you this is the place where Satan, again, tried to make an inroad against the battle plan. It is in the depths of thought that he will try to drag you away from truth. God has warned us not to totally trust even our own thoughts. But to take them and hold them up to the mirror of God's Word.

2 Corinthians 10:5

We demolish arguments and every pretension that sets itself up against the knowledge of God, and we take captive every thought to make it obedient to Christ.

Did you notice the word "pretension" in this verse? It's not a word that we use much anymore, but this is the word that God had me focus on at this point in the battle. It is from the

Greek word (epsoma) which means proud or arrogant. The verse is saying we need to be watching that our own thoughts and reasoning processes do not become more important to us than God's truth. We need to take hold of our thoughts and weigh them against what IS true, not against what we THINK or wish truth to be. Satan's plan from the Garden of Eden against Eve and in the desert against Christ included the boasting of what we have or what we can do. Truth is a possession; you either have it or you do not. If you have only a little truth, just enough to think you are in the right, the devil will work your pride persuading you to hold onto it with a white knuckled grip. We often hold onto our perspective as if we are the keepers of all truth, when the reality is that in any given conflict we have a thimble full information taken from an ocean of truth.

Taking every thought captive is a difficult undertaking. Most of us believe that every thought that comes to our mind originates within our own brain. I've come to the realization that this is not always true. Though most thoughts do originate within our minds, there are times when Satan, or members of his demon army whisper thoughts into what I like to refer to as, our "minds ear." You've heard of the "minds eye?" When you close your eyes and think of something you can picture it in your mind. I believe our mind also has hearing, and it is in our subconscious mind where the spiritual realm has its connection into our physical world. God speaks to us in our minds ear as many of you perhaps have heard this described as a "still small voice" (1 Kings 19:12). Evil can speak to us in this place as well. It is in the minds ear where evil injects lies into our thinking.

As I came to this step in the battle and worked through the truth of my situation it became more and more clear to me that all of what I was thinking did not originate from truthful thoughts on my part but from lies whispered to me in order to separate me from communion with God the Holy Spirit as well as the Body of Christ.

Within the battle it is important not to go running down the Flip Wilson road of theology; "The Devil made me do it!" For those of you who are younger than 40, go ask your mom or dad who Flip Wilson is. To gain proper perspective on Satan's plan in this area look at these verses from James:

James 1:14-16

...but each one is tempted when, by his own evil desire, he is dragged away and enticed. [15] Then, after desire has conceived, it gives birth to sin; and sin, when it is full-grown, gives birth to death. [16] Don't be deceived, my dear brothers.

These verses put the blame for sin squarely on the shoulders of the individual. We are responsible for any thoughts, words or actions which emanate from our mind. It is no different than someone standing next to us making a suggestion that we steal something, or say something degrading to someone or lie about someone. Even though the thought originated from the other person, it is our responsibility whether or not we act on their suggestion. When sin is suggested to us from an outside source, physical or spiritual, it is not ours until we begin to dwell on it. Once we embrace the suggestion and "desire" it, the suggestion has now become our own thought and our own responsibility. We need to take these thoughts captive and consider their validity, their origin and most importantly their truth. Step one, as I said, is difficult. But it will be the difference between resolving your difficult circumstance as quickly as possible, or dragging out a conflict for weeks, months, and all too often years. Stop and relentlessly pursue the truth of your circumstance.

Praying through these steps is so important. Communicate with God and ask Him to open your eyes to see things clearly. If you are having relational struggles, get a third party involved who can be trusted to insert complete truth into the situation. If you are having financial difficulties, seek counsel from someone who is good with money and will not be judgmental because you have made mistakes in this area. Whatever is causing you distress, I guarantee you are not seeing the truth, the whole truth and nothing but the truth of your circumstances. Take the challenge—seek truth.

Chapter Twelve "May I Take Your Order" has questions and note sections to help you walk through each step in the Battle Plan. These questions can be used to help an individual, a small group or a church body deal with whatever conflict they find themselves in. Once again I want to implore you to take the time needed to effectively work through this step. Seek wise counsel to help you sort through truth.

Chapter Five

Two Wrongs Don't Make a Right (But Three Lefts Do)

I have been asked to assemble all types of items over the years. If you are a father or husband, as I am, you know exactly what I am talking about. Whether it be Christmas presents, birthday presents or the purchase of a new barbecue grill, many times in our lives we have read those three words that strike fear in our very soul; "Some Assembly Required!"

Whatever the item, whether it be a toy, a piece of furniture or the afore mentioned grill, all of these things that require assembly have one very important commonality; The Instruction Manual. I remember on more that one occasion trying to assemble a toy or an entertainment center without following the instructions. Why would I do that? The ladies reading know the answer to that question. It's because I'm a man! It seemed so obvious to me how the assembling should go. These occasions have all ended the same way. Standing over the item holding a piece which requires me to dismantle what has already been assembled in order to place the small, but very important piece where it belongs. This always involves picking up the instruction manual and beginning with step one and following the directions to discover exactly where I went wrong. I then dismantle the item to the point of the error, and continue to reassemble the item in the proper way.

In life, God has given us a guide to show us a process that works. Of course, I am talking about The Bible. I once heard an acrostic used to describe the content of God's Word. B.I.B.L.E.—Basic Instructions Before Leaving Earth. This is not new and I am not even sure when or where I heard it for the first time. Even though this acrostic has been around for a long time I still share it because of the simple truth it reveals. God has given us guidelines to follow in life. His Word contains those instructions. The Bible speaks about areas such as finances, relationships, work, and parenting; just to name a few. The areas that we have been looking into is conflict and spiritual warfare. As you have already seen, the Scriptures speak to us about these areas as well. Satan does not want us to respond biblically to any circumstances that are causing turmoil, mistrust, disunity or division between those who love God. It doesn't matter if you were the source of the problem or if someone else was the source of the problem. If it involves you as a Christian, and the conflict is dragging on, you need to humble yourself and move toward righteousness. The reality is, if we stubbornly hold our ground, those looking on will begin to view God or His people in a negative way. Understanding this led me to realize that it was my responsibility to get into The Word of God and find the righteous response which will lead to restoration.

The word "Righteousness" is one of those words that have been labeled as a "church word" and people nod when they hear it, but not many people really know what it means. I wrote of this word earlier and now we will uncover the full biblical understanding of this often misunderstood word. Most think it means to be holy or perfect. That is only one part of its definition when it comes to the biblical perspective. We can never be righteous enough or do enough good things to earn salvation. We can only be deemed righteous through knowing and trusting Jesus as our personal Lord and Savior.

Titus 3:5
... *he saved us, not because of righteous things we had done, but because of his mercy.*

It is then that we receive what is called "imputed" righteousness. Imputed righteousness is having righteousness put on us. God, in His mercy, views us through the sacrifice and blood of Jesus Christ and sees us as righteous. But there is another biblical definition to this word which is connected to our actions and reactions. I wrote about this secondary definition in chapter three, the simplest meaning of the word righteousness is "to do things God's way." If we are living a righteous life we are believing what God says about our circumstances and in turn we do things God's way.

2 Timothy 3:16-17
All Scripture is God-breathed and is useful for teaching, rebuking, correcting and training in righteousness, so that the man of God may be thoroughly equipped for every good work.

Genesis 15:6
Abram believed the LORD, and he credited it to him as righteousness.

Walking in righteousness can be experienced by anyone who believes God. Titus 3:5 reveals to us that there are acts of righteousness apart from Salvation that can be done. These acts cannot save you in the sense of eternal salvation, but they can rescue you from harmful circumstances. This brings us to our second step. We have embraced step one by beginning and continuing the process of taking our thoughts captive, embracing what is true and dispelling whatever is not truth. This step needs to continue throughout the entire process. Satan will try to bring his lies at any and every point in order to distract us from drawing closer to the one who is truth.

The Second Step in The Battle Plan

Since righteousness is the second step in the Battle Plan, and the meaning of righteousness, in this context is to do things God's way, then our second step is clear. What does the Bible say about our circumstances, our situations, our responses, our attitudes, and our actions?

In my own situation, I had offended people. Even though it was not intentional, it still was my responsibility. What does God's Word say about that? I knew the answer already, but I will share the Scriptures that applied to my situation so you can make note in your own Bible.

Luke 17:3

So watch yourselves. "If your brother sins, rebuke him, and if he repents, forgive him.

There are two words in this text that we will need to take a closer look at. They are the words 'rebuke' and 'repent.' The word rebuke is translated from the Greek word (epitimeson). This word means to warn or to strongly admonish. In other words, tell them they messed up and tell them clearly so there is no doubt as to what you are saying. I believe I described this process in my situation using the term "shock and awe." I heard it clearly, and it hit me like a bomb! Don't misunderstand, it was not delivered harshly, it was delivered with love and care. But it was direct and with no possibility of misunderstanding. The shock and awe was due to the fact that I was TOTALLY unaware of my offenses. Since the 'rebuke' portion of God's process had already been completed, my responsibility was within the second portion of this verse and the second word we needed to research a little bit more. The word is 'repent.' Growing up I thought this word meant to be sorry for doing something wrong. As I've studied and grown in God's Word I have come to see that this word has a much deeper, action based meaning. Repent in the Greek is (metanoese) which certainly means to have regret, but it is much more than just feeling sorrow. It is to have regret with action. When we repent we turn from the negative or sinful action and move in a totally opposite direction. In other words stop doing the wrong thing and do the right thing.

The action that I needed to take, as soon as possible, was to let those who I had offended know that I am now aware of how I had made them feel, and then to ask for their forgiveness. I would also need to begin the work of changing those types of responses and actions which caused these hard feelings. My biggest fear was that I would try to justify my behavior within my apology. I was led to send an email to those whom I had offended, with the intent of speaking with each of them personally as God opened the doors of opportunity. If your particular circumstance involves only one person then a personal conversation, in most cases, is the best approach.

As I prayed, God impressed on my heart that I cannot just send an "I'm sorry" email. My response must reveal that I have been made aware of my specific behavior. My words and actions had offended them and made them feel squashed and apprehensive about giving an opinion or offering suggestions. I sought their forgiveness with no excuses.

Asking for forgiveness is something very different than just saying, "I'm sorry." I'm not talking about those times when you step on someone's toe or bump into someone accidentally. Of course, you can say I'm sorry in those circumstances. But even then, asking for forgiveness requires a response. In my opinion saying, "I'm sorry" is me letting myself off the hook. It requires no response on the part of the one to whom it is being said. On the other hand, when someone asks, "Will you forgive me?" This is a question that requires a response. You are leaving yourself in the hands of the offended. It requires humility to ask someone to forgive you.

The Bible uses the word and concept of asking for and seeking forgiveness literally hundreds of times. But it only uses the word "sorry" twice and one of those is describing pity, to feel sorry for someone. Seeking forgiveness and having a heart of forgiveness for others is a biblical principle that every true believer is called to live out. It is the very foundation of the gospel. This is not as easy as saying "I'm sorry." You will be leaving yourself at the mercy of the offended and there is no way to know how they will respond. You have probably already asked this question as you have been reading, "What if they will not forgive me?"

The biblical truth is this; your responsibility is to follow God's process. If you have come with true repentance and humility with a sincere request to be forgiven, then that is all you are responsible for. Their response will be their responsibility. But if they are following the same biblical process from the other side, then they have a responsibility also. Returning to the verse that called for our response, we can see what the response of the offended should be.

Luke 17:3 (bold mine)

So watch yourselves. "If your brother sins, rebuke him, ***and if he repents, forgive him.***

We are called to forgive. We do need to realize that depending on the severity of the sin and the offense, it may not be easy for the offended to forgive immediately. A lot of this will depend on your character, your sincerity and how effectively you processed the first step of truth. Just as it will be difficult for you to process and hold onto truth and keep Satan out of your mind and thoughts, the same will be true for those who have been offended. The Bible also speaks to those who have been offended.

Matthew 18:15-16

"If your brother sins against you, go and show him his fault, just between the two of you. If he listens to you, you have won your brother over. [16] But if he will not listen, take one or two others along, so that 'every matter may be established by the testimony of two or three witnesses.'

Satan will be in their thoughts and in their 'minds ear' whispering lies to keep truth from being pursued. He will whisper lies directing them not to speak **to** you, but to talk **about** you to others. They will hear lies directing them to totally disassociate with the one who offended them. They will hear lies saying the offender does not deserve forgiveness. If you have been offended, trust me when I tell you, the silent treatment never resolves an issue. I once tried the silent treatment on my wife. For three days I brooded and became more and more angry as I silently pouted and avoided her in an effort to make her pay for whatever it was she had done (I honestly don't even remember what it was—that's how insignificant it truly was). Finally I confronted her with the issue and it was all worked out within minutes. I then asked her if she even noticed I was giving her the silent treatment. To my dismay she had never even noticed I was angry. She jokingly said it was the most peaceful three days of her life. If you even think you may have offended someone, go to them and ask. Don't expect the offended to reveal their pain to you.

If it was you who had done the offending and rightly asked for forgiveness, do not be surprised if you do not receive an immediate response of forgiveness and hugs all around. Be prepared to NOT be forgiven immediately. This is a true test of a humble heart. Will you accept the possible response of "NO!" or "I don't forgive you!" Are you prepared to receive either of those responses and not be angry or judgmental toward that person? But trust them with God to work out their feelings, their journey, and their own personal righteousness. In most cases when we come humbly to those whom we have offended and seek forgiveness, forgiveness will be happily granted.

I have one final warning for you if you are preparing to approach someone to seek forgiveness. Ask yourself this very important question, "Am I expecting a positive response?" If you have not prepared yourself for at least the possibility of a negative response, then you are setting yourself up for a continuing attack by the enemy. People don't always meet our expectations; this is part of the truth you need to be processing. Be prepared to receive the worst FROM them and still leave thinking the best OF them.

You've taken step one in the Battle Plan and you have prayerfully discovered the truth within your particular circumstance. Hopefully you have also recognized your part in the conflict. You've taken those thoughts captive and weigh them against God's Word. How does God's Word instruct you to respond? I will warn you ahead of time; you may disagree with God's way and want to try things your own way. However, taking three left turns is not the same as taking one right turn. You may need to take some time to pray and ask God about His Ways. Along those lines, I would like to give you a direction for your prayers to help you avoid some wasted time. *Forget about asking God to see it your way, the Bible is not going to change.* I give this advice out of experience. Begin by asking God to change your heart in order for you to trust that His way is best. Now you are on the path toward righteousness. Knowing how to respond in every situation is not righteousness. Believing that God knows how we should respond in every situation then following His direction—that is righteousness.

Genesis 15:6

Abram believed the LORD, and he credited it to him as righteousness.

One final thought on forgiveness. I have discovered the most difficult person to forgive is ourselves. If we have hurt, offended or sinned against someone it is important to stick to the Battle Plan and follow the steps of truth and righteousness, which leads to forgiveness and reconciliation. This next sentence is so important. If you have recognized your sin, confessed it before God, and sought out forgiveness from those whom you have offended, whether they forgive you or not is not as important as your being able to forgive yourself. Did you discover the whole truth of your circumstances? Did you find your righteous, biblical response and then follow through with it? Then the forgiveness you seek from God has been given. If those who have received your request for forgiveness are obeying the Word of God, they will in time grant forgiveness. You should be just as willing to grant this same forgiveness to yourself. Forgiving yourself is the doorway to freedom. Satan will try to whisper lies into your mind. He will try to tell you, "You are not forgiven" or that God could never forgive sins as terrible as the ones you have committed. These thoughts are not truth! God's truth is this:

1 John 1:9

If we confess our sins, he is faithful and just and will forgive us our sins and purify us from all unrighteousness.

Have we truthfully confessed our sins before God? Have we responded in righteousness when it comes to those who we have sinned against? If the answer to both of those questions is "yes" then 1 John 1:9 is directed to us. Embrace forgiveness and the peace and freedom that are rightfully yours from our Heavenly Father.

Chapter Six

A "Peace" of the Action (Hold the phone—It's a homophone)

During those years I worked as a Correction Officer I was also involved in the Tactical Response Team (TRT). This was a team of about fifty men and women who were specially trained to respond to riots and large scale inmate insurrections. Most of you watch the news on television and have seen police officers dressed in riot gear controlling large crowds. That is essentially what the TRT was trained to do. The only difference is, our training was specific to cell blocks, prison yards and every other location where a large group problem could occur within the walls of a prison.

Every large Institution in Massachusetts has its own TRT, and once a year all the teams would come together for a day of training, demonstration and competition. During my time with the TRT, I participated in several of these competitions. One of the side benefits of these gatherings was that every team was learning and training to do the same things, to respond to the same commands, and work as one enormous team. Oh yah! The food was great too!

We often wondered why we had to do this annual training and demonstration day with all of these other Tactical Response Teams, then the day came when we realized why this type of preparation was necessary.

I went to work like any other day. I don't recall anything happening out of the ordinary except we did get word that some kind of problem was going on at the Norfolk Prison, and it involved a large group of inmates. Other than that we had no other information. As the day ended I was headed to the exit of the prison when the entire day shift was held at the exit. We were told that the trouble at Norfolk had escalated and Norfolk's TRT was not big enough to handle the number of inmates involved. Then the order went out to our shift. All TRT members are now activated and ordered to report to Norfolk and await further instructions. I had been involved in a few smaller problems that were easily handled by our team at the Bridgewater Prison complex, but this sounded much bigger. Norfolk had a very large and well trained team, and if this uprising was beyond their capacity, just how big was it? I could feel my adrenaline begin to rise as I drove to the TRT equipment storage building to retrieve my equipment. After a brief meeting with the first responding TRT members from Bridgewater, we loaded our bus with equipment and personnel, and headed to Norfolk where the remainder of the team would meet us at the assembling point. As our team arrived we could see that just about every team in the state had been activated. Team after team arrived at the training facility just outside of the Norfolk prison walls. My excitement for a piece of the action slowly began to turn into anxiety and apprehension. Our team commander went to the Command Center for an update and plan of action as we waited for what seemed like hours for information about the inevitable confrontation. We soon would learn that within the walls were several hundred inmates in the yard. They were refusing to return to their cells and were threatening to kill anyone who came into the yard. All non-security staff had been evacuated safely and the immediate plan was to test their resolve with time. We would let them stay in the yard all night and strategically overwhelm them at daybreak by sending every Tactical Response Team flooding into the yard from predetermined strategic entrances.

The long wait for daybreak seemed endless. I tried to get some rest but sleep evaded me. Finally, just before dawn each team assembled in formation in front of the Command Center. The mission commander stood before us and began to disseminate our orders for the plan of attack. It was in that moment, as the plan was being laid out, I heard something that made my heart jump into my throat. The Bridgewater team would be the first team through the main entrance to the yard. My heart jumped because I was the squad leader of squad-one. I'm sure you have quickly surmised that I was one of the first Officers into the yard. Along with my TRT Commander and Lieutenant Commander, I led my team through the double doors into the inmate yard. I could feel my heart pounding against my chest like a base drum. My eyes were wide open and I was fully anticipating a wave of aggressive inmates attacking my team within moments of entering the yard. However, the reality was something quite different. The inmates were in the center of the yard about thirty or forty yards from where we entered. The shock of seeing our team, as well as all the other teams that kept pouring into the yard from every available entrance, sent the inmates scurrying for cover like roaches when the lights are turned on! The inmates where purposely given only one escape route which led them all into a small room that barely held them all. The door was closed and secured, and the inmates could then be taken out one-by-one and reclassified to a higher security facility.

I cannot even begin to tell you the sense of peace that overwhelmed me as I entered the yard and not only saw the inmates were not armed and ready to attack but that they were cold, hungry, confused and running in fear. The intelligence the commanders had received was accurate and the plan of attack was incredibly successful.

Wouldn't you like to have that kind of intelligence against your enemy, the devil? Wouldn't it be great to have the kind of information that would cause him and his army to scurry for cover like roaches when the lights are turned on?

The Battle has been put into action. Steps One and Two have been completed. We have examined our actions and our thoughts through the prism of truth and hopefully have come to a place where all lies are being recognized and discarded. We have realized that God has called us to respond by doing things His way, whatever that means in our particular set of circumstances. If you have seen the truth, and have acted in righteousness, then you are ready for the next step.

The Third Step in The Battle Plan

It may be difficult to see at first, but Peace is a very important part of this Battle Plan. It is the third step you will be taking. To be more precise, Ephesians 6:15 actually calls it the "gospel of peace."

As I mentioned earlier the word "gospel" literally translates "good news." Within Christian circles, when someone says "the gospel," it instantly brings the believer's mind to a specific type of "good news." The specific type of good news that Christians think of is the good news of Jesus paying our penalty by dying on the cross for our sins, being buried and rising again on the third day, thereby conquering sin and death. Now I am not trying to tell you that this is not good news, because this is clearly the best news that a lost world could ever hear. What I am trying to convey is that every time the Greek word (evangeliou) is used in the Bible it may not be speaking about that specific good news. Ephesians 6:15 is one of those instances. In fact, this verse actually identifies what the good news is. It is the good news "of peace." Within the Salvation Plan this peace is with God. But as we transition into a Battle Plan this peace becomes a very important part of our defense. Sometimes when we read the Bible, we make things much harder than they actually are.

Just as my heart stopped pounding and my tension subsided as I entered that prison yard and watched those inmates flee, you too can experience that sense of immediate peace as you realize your attitudes and actions have caused Satan to flee. This becomes a point of confirmation and as well as an avenue to continue with the Battle Plan.

James 4:5-7

Or do you think Scripture says without reason that the spirit he caused to live in us envies intensely? 6 But he gives us more grace. That is why Scripture says: "God opposes the proud but gives grace to the humble." {6 Prov. 3:34} 7 Submit yourselves, then, to God. Resist the devil, and he will flee from you.

The Holy Spirit within us wants our spirit to connect with only Him. He does not want our spirit to even be available to hear the lies that the devil and the demons want to whisper in our ear. He is jealous and He envies intensely any connections we have with anything other than Him. The Holy Spirit within us is that third part of the eternal, triune God. Come to God with a humble heart. Totally tune out and eliminate those things that allow your spirit to be distracted from an uninterrupted connection with the Holy Spirit, who took up residence within you the moment you cried out to the Savior for forgiveness. The result of that kind of submission is the devil and his evil minions scurrying for cover. As Satan leaves your presence, you will be overwhelmed with an amazing sense of peace. Now isn't that good news?

Romans 5:1

Therefore, since we have been justified through faith, we have peace with God through our Lord Jesus Christ,

When my team entered that yard we were putting our trust in those who could see more and had more information than we did. We were given a clear and precise plan for entering into battle. Because we executed the plan we were given, the results were immediate, obvious and gratifying. God can see more and has far more information than we do. Why would we continue to try to execute our own battle plan, or even worse not even admit that we are in a battle?

In my own circumstances I experienced this peace after taking the action I knew was God's best. After I weighed through the morass of Satan's lies, I began to see myself through the prism of truth. I then was profoundly aware of how God wanted me to respond. But it wasn't until I began to walk in that righteousness (do things God's way) that I would begin to receive the good news of peace. The peace I experienced motivated me to continue to execute God's Battle Plan. God was assuring me that complete peace in this area of my life was attainable if I would trust His plan. Admittedly, I did not have a total sense of the specific outcome at that moment, but the realization of the possibilities was added strength to continue through the steps and fully motivated my forward motion.

Psalm 119:105
Your word is a lamp to my feet and a light for my path.

God's Word tells us that we are in a struggle, a battle, an unseen war. Embrace His plan to freedom and the peace that comes from unity with the Holy Spirit within us. The third action step is to pursue the peace that comes from responding God's way and cultivating an exclusive relationship with the Holy Spirit. All thoughts and actions are brought into this relationship before they are enacted. Peace will be our strength when we know that God is directing our path.

Chapter Seven

A Slap in The Faith (Thanks—I Needed That)

As a Correction Officer I experienced so many scenarios that my training officers never prepared me for. The right thing to do was not etched in stone; it wasn't written in a manual and it was never addressed at roll call. It is in these moments that I would put my faith in God, and my experience into action, trusting that the outcome would be good. I remember one such moment during a day that I was working a double shift. On my second shift after the evening meal I was assigned as the Gym Officer. My duties, in general, were to simply observe all the activities going on in the gym and in the inmate yard, which was just outside of the gym. Just before the final call for inmates to return to their cell blocks, I was walking past the weight lifting area where there were only two inmates left finishing up their work-out. The one inmate who was finished asked me how much I could bench press. I simply smiled at him and said, "don't worry about how much I can lift." He laughed and replied, "You probably can't even lift your own body weight." The inmate continued, "You look like you weigh about one-eighty," (He was close—but that was a long time ago) As he loaded one hundred and seventy-five pounds onto the bar, he turned to me again, "That's one seventy-five, close enough, get on the bench and prove me wrong." I noticed that the other inmate, with whom I had a good rapport, was watching and waiting for my response. However, he seemed concerned, not amused at all by the taunts of his friend. I turned to the inmate who was taunting me and replied to him as I grinned, "You seem to think I need to prove something to you." He smiled and asked, "So you can't lift it?" I answered him once again, "You want to see whether or not I can lift the weight, but I already know the answer, so I have nothing to prove." His final words as he walked away were these, "You can't lift it! You can't lift it!"

The other inmate got up and actually looked upset at what his friend had done. I guess in his eyes I had been shown up. Just before the second inmate left the gym, I called him back to where I was near the bench press. There was no one else in the gym except us. The weights were still on the bar and the bar was still set up on the bench. I told him that I noticed he was bothered by what the other guy had said to me, and I assured him that his taunts didn't bother me. He said to me, "I just hate it when guys who are strong pick on guys who are not as strong as them."

I asked him, "What makes you think I am not as strong as him?" He replied tentatively, "Well, you didn't lift it, so I just assumed that you can't." I sat down on the bench and looked that inmate right in the eyes and said, "I do this only for you, because you have always been very respectful to me, but if you tell anyone about this—I will deny it." I laid down on the bench reached up and lifted the bar off the rack and slowly lowered the one hundred and seventy-five pounds down onto my chest. I glanced over to see the inmate's eyes wide open awaiting my arms to press the weight back up to its position. He looked like he was ready to run over and grab the bar that he was obviously expecting to fall back onto my chest. I then lifted it back up, arms straight and looked back at him, and he smiled. But I didn't stop with one lift! I proceeded to lift the weight five more times before gently placing the bar back on the rack. The inmate stood staring with his mouth wide open, "Wow! I never expected that! You are way stronger than you look!" He turned to leave and quickly spun around to ask me one last question, "Why didn't you just do that and shut that guy up?" I smiled and said, "Because, he's an idiot!" He turned again to leave and said, "You're right, he is an idiot!"

When we train to be Correction Officers, one of the most important pieces of information conveyed to us is that we must not allow ourselves to be distracted from our duties by inmates who are taunting, or even just speaking to us as we work. I was very aware of that truth when the first inmate was trying to get me to engage in lifting the weights. However, with the second inmate I let myself be led by another factor; my experience and knowledge told me that this inmate was different and needed to see a different side of me. He needed to see a trusting side, a confident side, and a strong side.

My insights were rewarded months later when I encountered a problem with several inmates on a block. That same inmate from the gym stepped in and stood beside me, and the other inmates involved backed down because of his reputation in the prison. He said to them, "I've seen this guy in action, you don't know what you're getting yourselves into." The other inmates backed down out of respect for him.

When I asked him why he did that, his answer very much surprised me. He said, "That day in the gym, you made me think about how I am always worried about what others think of me. You taught me something that day, and you respected me enough to show me who you really are. And I'm not talking about how strong you are. That meant a lot to me."

The Fourth Step in The Battle Plan

If we have come through a difficult time in life and begin to act on God's Battle Plan, the result is the strength and confidence that comes with Faith. We discovered truth, searched for righteousness and we've been comforted and motivated with peace. The peace that we embrace will bring us to the fourth step in the plan, which is faith. I've discovered that faith is actually both a result as well as a decisive step. When I embraced the third step of peace and the strength it brings, my faith in what God could do seemed to be a natural byproduct. But I came to see that continuing to walk in that faith requires a purposeful decision on my part. For faith to be effective for those of us who are actively in the battle it must move us to action.

I have said many times throughout this book that Satan will try to distract you at every step. This step is no different. Trusting God with who you are becoming, and walking in the faith that He has brought you to, is not just for you, but also to display your source of strength to others. Our journey in life is seldom just for us. God does want each of us, individually, to grow and be drawn closer to Him each day. But built into our journey is the journey of each and every person we interact with in life.

The second inmate's perspective was changed. But not just his perspective of me, his perspective of himself was changed as well. That is what this step of faith can do. Don't just be content in being out of the darkness. Be part of the light for those people you know who are also in a time of darkness. I was in a position to share my journey with three or four hundred people in a message I gave at Lifecoast Church. That was part of my faith step. Having the faith that God can use my pain, my dark hours and even my bad responses to encourage and help others through their own pain. As I said, the evil one does not want us to grow in our faith. He began a siege of lies on that Sunday morning trying to get me to believe that a pastor who shares failure is a failure as a pastor. I knew from walking through God's Battle Plan that faith needs to be shared. If we have responded to our failures in righteousness, then God can turn them into successes. In your faith step you need to find a way to share your journey, whether it is with a friend, a group of friends, or some kind of small group through your church. Sharing your journey puts faith into action. It says I am trusting God that my pain and heartache had purpose in my life, and in the lives of those around me.

2 Corinthians 12:10

That is why, for Christ's sake, I delight in weaknesses, in insults, in hardships, in persecutions, in difficulties. For when I am weak, then I am strong.

Your persistent faith through difficult and dark times can be the greatest strength to those who have watched you through your weakness to continually put your faith in God for the outcome. That is why this step is so difficult to maintain. Satan does not want faith to grow and spread. He knows all too well that faith grown out of weakness is a faith not easily shaken. A faith that has been born out of a life of ease can be attacked at the foundation. If we believe that God will never let anything bad happen to us, then we are building our trust on a shaky foundation. We are setting ourselves up for failure. Even Jesus told us that we would have trouble.

John 16:33

"I have told you these things, so that in me you may have peace. In this world you will have trouble. But take heart! I have overcome the world."

Somewhere along the road of history, someone decided to share a different gospel than the one that Jesus gave us. A gospel that says we will have no trouble, no sickness and no stress. That conclusion can only be gleaned from Scripture if you take a selective reading approach to the Bible. A life without failure, without insults, without hardship, without persecution and without difficulties is a life that has never truly understood the true depths of faith and its power to overcome those things and impact others for the kingdom of God.

Hebrews 11:1

Now faith is being sure of what we hope for and certain of what we do not see.

Our faith will grow, as we trust God through our pain and difficult circumstances. We trust that He will complete His work in and through us. A mature faith says that no matter the outcome I will trust God with the greater purpose of His plan. Even if I cannot see it's direction or understand its purpose at this moment.

Philippians 1:6

...being confident of this, that he who began a good work in you will carry it on to completion until the day of Christ Jesus.

During this step in the Battle Plan we need to turn our heart and thoughts toward a Savior that is continuing His work. As we trust Him for His result, our anxiety, our stress, our pain and our urges to run or lash out will subside in the reality of a greater purpose. It is during this time of increased faith that the next step will begin to be revealed to you.

Chapter Eight

Somebody Save Me!
(Knock, Knock. Who's there? Dwayne! Dwayne who? Dwayne the bathtub, I'm Dwowning!)

A fire inside a prison can be even more dangerous than a fire in a public building. In a prison, most of the doors are locked and the inmates are at the mercy of the Correctional Staff who control the exits, not just to the outside, but from one area to the next. A fire in a cell block or cell corridor can be the most dangerous, not only because of the flames, but because of the smoke which has no where to go and will quickly consume the oxygen in the block, corridor and more dangerously the cells. In a prison fire the probability is much, much higher for inmates or officers to die from smoke inhalation than from any burn related injury.

In 1984, while working on the day shift, I recall hearing the fire alarm system while at my post on a third floor corridor station. My phone immediately rang and as I answered it the Control Center informed me that the alarm indicator had been activated on a 4th floor corridor which was two or three corridors away from my post. I ran to the fourth floor and unlocked the large, solid door that separated the corridors. I was met by a wall of smoke and all I could hear were inmates kicking their doors and screaming to be let out. I left the corridor door opened, radioed the Control Center with my location and the situation, and began to unlock the cells of a long, eighteen cell corridor, which was totally filled with smoke. I had unlocked only two or three cells before I was overcome with smoke myself. I had to stick my face up against the bars of the outside wall windows to get some fresh air into my lungs. I took two or three deep breaths, held my breath and unlocked two or three more cells and retreated to a window again and repeated the process until all the inmates were removed from the corridor. In the last cell of the corridor it was discovered that the cause of all the smoke was a mattress, which had been ignited by a cigarette. An hour earlier an inmate had lit the cigarette and dropped it when he had nodded off while waiting for his cell to be unlocked so he could go to work in the kitchen. He was awakened abruptly and left his cell quickly, completely forgetting about the cigarette.

During that response, I will never forget the expressions on the faces of those inmates as I unlocked their cell doors and gave them access to safety. The sense of relief on their faces and the expressions of gratitude toward me were genuine. There is no mistaking the response of a person who has experienced salvation. It doesn't matter if the salvation is physical or spiritual, if they have truly experienced salvation, the response is obvious.

The word "salvation" in the Greek is (soterian) and it has a broad range of meanings. It can mean salvation as most Christians understand it; salvation from eternal punishment by calling on the name of Jesus asking for, and receiving forgiveness from sin. Anyone can receive salvation by trusting that Jesus' death, burial and resurrection paid the penalty for their sin. To put it more succinctly, if we have experienced

"Salvation" we have been saved from an eternity in Hell, and have received an eternity with God. But within Scripture this is not the only meaning of the word "soterian." It can also mean to be physically rescued or delivered from your circumstances, pain or state of mind. So it is important to look at the context of each passage and take its correct, contextual meaning. This, of course is true of any word or verse found in the Bible.

The Fifth Step in The Battle Plan

When we read the word 'salvation' as part of the Battle Plan we must look at it as deliverance or a rescue from our circumstances. As you walk through each step the result will be a victory, or being successful against the attack the enemy has been waging. You will begin by discovering the truth about yourself or the situation you found yourself in. You then will take the next step of righteousness and align your actions according to what the Bible says about you and/or your particular struggle. Peace for yourself, as well as the peace you bring to the conflict, will be the result of the steps taken from obedience found in God's Word. These important steps in the Battle Plan will cause the enemy to flee. The result will be the bolstering of your faith in God and the truth of His Word. Your faith will grow and move you to action, which is protection for you and others from similar attacks by the enemy. We will soon realize, as a result of these steps we have taken, we have been delivered from the attack of the enemy. Not only will you experienced a victory in the battle, but you will also discover this salvation is something that can be taught and shared. As you take the time to honestly walk through each step, you will experience salvation from physical and psychological holds which had been placed on you from the spiritual realm.

In my own crisis I was able to move forward in ministry. Admittedly, there were still barriers that had to be overcome. Regaining trust, feeling safe to share openly, as well as allowing others to feel safe in sharing with me, were just a few of the hurdles which had to be overcome. Even though the spiritual attacks may cease, the reality is there will still be battle wounds that will require time to fully heal.

Similarly, those men in the corridor during that prison fire, though they experienced salvation from the circumstances, it still took several hours for them to breath free and easy after inhaling so much smoke. But as long as they allowed fresh air to continue going in and out of their lungs, they soon were breathing normally again.

In your situation, once you have gone through each step to the point of salvation, you will need to move toward reestablishing relationships again, hopefully sooner than later. The longer you wait to reconcile the relationship the more difficult it will become. There will be awkwardness, there will be uncomfortability. But now you will be going in with your eyes open, your heart and mind will be ready to ward off any attacks aimed at your thoughts.

My suggestion is that you talk about the eight hundred pound gorilla in the room! Don't just feel the awkwardness, talk about it to those with whom you've just reconciled. Remember, when truth is spoken Satan will flee. He cannot be in the presence of truth. Truth and lies cannot occupy the same space.

James 4:6-7

That is why Scripture says: "God opposes the proud but gives grace to the humble." Submit yourselves, then, to God. Resist the devil, and he will flee from you.

If we humble ourselves before both God and those whom we have offended or even those who have offended us, the resulting truth which now is the foundation for the relationship will cause the devil to abandon his attacks, and everyone will be breathing free and easy. Everyone involved can experience a sense of salvation from the conflict.

Perhaps your relationships have suffered greatly from the conflict. In your hearts you cannot see the affected relationships ever returning to what they once were. That may be true but I believe that through these steps each of you can come to a place where God can recreate a new and better relationship. It may never be what it was, but our God is able to make all things new.

Ephesians 4:22-24

You were taught, with regard to your former way of life, to put off your old self, which is being corrupted by its deceitful desires; to be made new in the attitude of your minds; and to put on the new self, created to be like God in true righteousness and holiness.

Chapter Nine

Word!
(Need I Say More?)

Each year in the Department of Correction every Officer is scheduled for a week of training. No one ever seems to be very enthusiastic about their training week. I think it stems from that old saying, "The only people who like change are wet babies." Some Officers enjoy the change in routine but most don't appear to like it at all. The training week consists of self-defense training, extraction training, First Aid & CPR, team building, firearms qualification, tear gas and pepper spray qualification and report writing. The list could go on and on, but you get the idea.

As you have probably surmised from the list, some of the classes are lecture style and some of them are interactive. But almost all of them are nearly the same information which you received the year before. You can imagine that after ten or fifteen years you may fail to see the need in attending a report writing class when you have been writing reports regularly day after day, week after week, and month after month. Less than enthusiastic is the kindest way to describe the attitudes of the officers who attend training week.

During those years of annual training, the benefits of repetitive training made its purpose very clear to me in my professional life as well as my personal life. On one occasion while working in the inmate mess hall, I observed an inmate stand up quickly, grab his throat and begin to run with a look of sheer panic on his face. An Officer from the other side of the room yelled, as the inmate began to run right toward the building exit, "Stop him! He's choking!" As the inmate approached me I tried to stop him but he was frantically trying to get by me and through the exit door. Since he had a running start it was difficult for me to slow his momentum, and we both went careening through the door to the outside walkway. Slowing his momentum while simultaneously ordering him to stop struggling, I was finally able to bring him to a complete stop. Without thinking, I turned him around, placed my arms under his arms, reached around his body and performed the Heimlich maneuver multiple times. On the third abdominal thrust a large piece of food shot out of his mouth and landed in the grass about eight feet from where we were standing. I think it was a hot dog! (I know, that's gross!) During those moments of fast action with only seconds to make a decision I realized I never stopped to try to remember what to do, I just did it! Those many weeks of training for the same procedures and methods had impressed in my mind the right thing to do when an emergency occurs. There was no delay trying to recall the right response for the situation. I simply reacted the way I had been trained to react.

On that day a young man's life was saved and I received a commendation for my fast action and professionalism.

Similarly, on two separate occasions in my personal life, two infants were saved because of the very same training. One of them was my own son Adam and the other was Caleb, the son of dear and precious friends. In each instance the infant was choking on something he had put in his mouth. Without thought I lifted the baby, turned him over and upside down with one hand to supporting his neck and head. I then performed a size appropriate back blow with the other hand. In both cases the object came flying out of the baby's mouth, along with the contents of their stomach (I know that's gross—again!). Watching those two boys grow up has been the greatest commendation I could ever receive. Adam is now 22 years old and Caleb is 18.

If we want to know how to act and react in life, we must receive regular training on how and when to use the appropriate responses we have learned. Just like the three situations previously mentioned, it would have been dangerous and potentially lethal for me to use the same method for the infants as I did for the choking adult. Just knowing a response does not mean you are fully trained. This brings us to our final step.

The Sixth Step in The Battle Plan

Take up the sword of the spirit, which is the Word of God. Just because you are not involved in a conflict now does not mean that you shouldn't be prepared. A conflict could be just around the corner waiting to introduce itself to you and throw your life into a tail spin. As I attended those training weeks year after year, I was sure that I didn't need to be there. But those three incidences, as well as many others, proved to me that training is a necessary part of learning how to respond properly when confronted with the unexpected. The best training manual we have to prepare us for the spiritually unexpected is the Word of God.

In Ephesians chapter 6 the Greek term, which is translated as "word", is (rhema). This is a very different term from (logos) which is also translated as "word" in other portions of the Bible. The term "logos" is used in John 1:1-2

John 1:1-2

In the beginning was the Word, and the Word was with God, and the Word was God. [2] *He was with God in the beginning.*

Logos is used in reference to Jesus as the Living Word of God and it is also used when describing the Bible as a whole, the Written Word of God. The term "logos" conveys the special manifestation of that which is both divine and human. The Bible is divine in that it is God breathed or God inspired yet human hands penned it. God divinely moved prophets, kings, apostles and apprentices as they incorporated their own writing styles yet still conveyed the precise message as the Holy Spirit directed them.

2 Peter 1:21

For prophecy never had its origin in the human will, but prophets, though human, spoke from God as they were carried along by the Holy Spirit.

2 Timothy 3:16—17

All Scripture is God-breathed and is useful for teaching, rebuking, correcting and training in righteousness, so that the man of God may be thoroughly equipped for every good work.

In similar fashion Jesus came from the glory of heaven and while being fully human never ceased to continue to be fully God.

Philippians 2:6-7

Who, being in very nature God, did not consider equality with God something to be grasped, [7] but made himself nothing, taking the very nature of a servant, being made in human likeness.

However the (rhema) of God conveys something very different. The (rhema) is the spoken word, the messages and the teachings of God. You might even say it is the spoken truth of God. There are many, many (rhemas) within the (logos) of God. It is like having an entire arsenal of weaponry.

It is vitally important to discover the teachings and truths of God. If we devote ourselves to discovering what God's Word says about our circumstance, there will be no conflict that is beyond our ability to handle. When we work through our conflicts, using the Word of God as our training guide, we become better equipped to handle the battle the next time it comes around. Our spiritual eyes recognize it immediately; our mind is now trained to respond spiritually as opposed to acting naturally. Our natural instinct, as I demonstrated earlier, is to Lie, Cry, Deny and Justify. These are the building blocks to division.

Jude 1:19

These are the men who divide you, who follow mere natural instincts and do not have the Spirit.

Our training in the Word should be ongoing and reinforced by those who fight along side us on the battleground. Training once a month, or only once a week on a Sunday morning at 10:00 a.m. is not a steady enough diet of instruction and encouragement to make one prepared for the spiritual onslaught that every believer will encounter. Every believer needs a wide scope of ongoing training to be fully prepared for the kingdom. Just like my training in the D.O.C., biblical training will fully prepare you for the work of the ministry. The training consists of many formats; Interactive, Full Contact, Lecture Style (Sitting and Listening), On the Job Training, Observation, and most importantly Reading and Studying. I'm sure you have seen, as I have, many great men and women of God have lost their influence and position because of one weak moment. We cannot afford to leave each other out there alone on the battle field.

1 Peter 5:8
Be self-controlled and alert. Your enemy the devil prowls around like a roaring lion looking for someone to devour.

The other part of training is proper application of instruction. Many people are well fed in the Word, but malnourished in application. In Matthew Chapter 4 Jesus was led by the Spirit into the desert to be tempted by Satan. When the temptation began Jesus immediately recognized Satan's plan of attack and used the "rhema" of God to win the battle. Jesus quoted Scripture. He Spoke the truths from scripture. If you recall, this was covered in chapter 2 (Modus Operandi). Jesus was demonstrating to us the divine battle plan, which we all need to devote ourselves to in order to protect ourselves against the enemy.

This is how Jesus responded to Satan in the desert. Every time the devil tempted Jesus from his time tested temptation plan, Jesus responded with God's opposing truth.

Mathew 4:2-4

After fasting forty days and forty nights, he was hungry. The tempter came to him and said, "If you are the Son of God, tell these stones to become bread." Jesus answered, "It is written:

'Man shall not live on bread alone, but on every word that comes from the mouth of God.

Jesus' reply was from Deuteronomy 8:3. Each of his responses to the devil's temptations were the "rhema," the spoke Word of God. When we are in conflict Satan will invade our thoughts with lies about the people we are in conflict with. But he doesn't stop there. The devil will continue to try to feed us a steady diet of lies about ourselves as well. Our offensive weapon is the Word of God. This is given to us as "rhema" because there are different truth responses for each and every attack. We must counter each lie with its opposing Biblical truth. If the lie of getting revenge comes into our mind we must respond with God's opposing truth.

Romans 12:19

Do not take revenge, my dear friends, but leave room for God's wrath, for it is written: "It is mine to avenge; I will repay," says the Lord.

Are you equipped to respond with the spoken truth of God's Word? We all need to be diligent in learning the truths of the bible in order to be equipped to fight back in this spiritual battle.

Where are you receiving your biblical instruction? Do you devote yourself to learn, not just the Word, but also the proper application of the Word? This is the area where instructors need to be trustworthy and held to account. Our teachers and trainers should be held to a standard of higher accountability.

James 3:1

Not many of you should presume to be teachers, my brothers, because you know that we who teach will be judged more strictly.

The lives of those who train us should be an open book. No secrets; no double standards! Our pastors and teachers must present honest hearts willing to identify and reveal their own short comings as they strive to be better leaders and students of the Word.

2 Peter 2:1

But there were also false prophets among the people, just as there will be false teachers among you. They will secretly introduce destructive heresies, even denying the sovereign Lord

As I implore you to be learning the Word under authority I also warn you to be diligent in whom you place your trust. Pray and seek the Spirits guidance.

Not surprisingly, part of Satan's battle plan is misdirection. If we learn the Word but never learn how to properly apply it in our lives or in the lives of those we encounter each day, the effects could be devastating.

Ephesians 4:11-14

It was he who gave some to be apostles, some to be prophets, some to be evangelists, and some to be pastors and teachers, to prepare God's people for works of service, so that the body of Christ may be built up until we all reach unity in the faith and in the knowledge of the Son of God and become mature, attaining to the whole measure of the fullness of Christ. Then we will no longer be infants, tossed back and forth by the waves, and blown here and there by every wind of teaching and by the cunning and craftiness of men in their deceitful scheming.

Be encouraged in knowing that God has appointed people to teach and train the body. Use your spiritual eyes, pray and ask those who you know and trust to direct you to those whom God has appointed to be apostles, evangelist, prophets, pastors and teachers. This journey was never meant to be traveled alone. This battle was never meant to be a boxing match. We are soldiers in the army of the King. In this war we must be alert never wandering from the protection of our unit.

Hebrews 10:23-25

Let us hold unswervingly to the hope we profess, for he who promised is faithful. [24] *And let us consider how we may spur one another on toward love and good deeds.* [25] *Let us not give up meeting together, as some are in the habit of doing, but let us encourage one another—and all the more as you see the Day approaching.*

Chapter Ten

Do You Pray? Or Are You Prey?
(One is BEFORE the meal the other IS the meal)

I'm sure you were wondering if I could weave a prison story into the topic of prayer. Well, I'm happy to say that I have yet another story! This one is not as exciting or glamorous as some of the other stories, but I think it will serve us well in demonstrating the point I am trying to make.

Every Correction Officer wears a two-way radio. The radio is equipped with a body alarm, as well as a cord connected speaker/microphone. The radio is designed to be held in a case on the officer's belt with the speaker/microphone extending up and clipping onto the lapel of the officer's uniform shirt. Why do I take the time to describe something most people have seen on their community police officer? I want you to get a mental picture of a person always having a speaker and a microphone conveniently available at all times.

One day I was working as the Corridor Sergeant. The Corridor Sgt. is responsible for all the cellblocks as well as any other areas connected to his corridor. Part of my job was to periodically make a trip through the counseling offices to maintain the safety of the counselors who met with inmates in that area. On this particular day I stopped in the office of a counselor who I had worked with for many years. She was not interviewing an inmate at the time and soon we were involved in a conversation. We hadn't seen each other in a while and I sat down to continue the conversation. After several minutes of discussing vacations, family and what we had planned for our days off, her office phone rang. She answered it and proceeded to inform me that our conversation was being broadcast to every officer with a radio (which is all of them). While sitting down, the arm on the chair pushed on the microphone button of the radio on my belt.

Are you seeing where I'm gong with this? Prayer is like wearing a heavenly two way radio. It is always available; it hears what you say and can be listened to for important information. Unless, like the story I told, we are holding down our transmit button and we are unable or unwilling to stop talking long enough to listen.

We are to approach our communication with God as if we were wearing a two way radio. A "pray-dio" if you will (sorry, that was bad). Seriously though, to take this approach to prayer brings a perspective that brings God into our daily lives in a way that we may have thought was impossible. If you are a Christian who has spent any consistent time in the Word of God, you are certainly aware of this verse; *I Thessalonians 5:17; Pray continually.*

If we take the radio concept to the application of this verse, we can clearly begin to become aware of our constant connection to God. We can speak to Him whenever we want or need to and He can speak to us. The other side of this application which may not be as comforting to realize is that God is listening even when we are not honoring Him or others with our conversation.

This prayer communication can and should be our greatest asset in The Battle Plan against thrones, rulers, powers and authorities in the spiritual realm. We have the power of prayer as the first line of defense in our arsenal of weaponry. This entire battle is, all too often, being fought without any communication. Too many allow their radios to be turned off. They decide from the natural how to fight a spiritual opponent. I cannot implore you enough to begin making decisions about spiritual matters from a spiritual perspective. Communicate with our Creator from a heart of worship and trust.

John 4:23-24
...a time is coming and has now come when the true worshipers will worship the Father in spirit and truth, for they are the kind of worshipers the Father seeks. God is spirit, and his worshipers must worship in spirit and in truth."

Satan desires to devour us. He looks at us like a lion looks at its prey. If we would only pray we wouldn't become prey. Our perspective of people, circumstances and yes even conflict would totally change if we would live and have our being in a constant attitude and understanding of continually communicating with God. If, when someone offends you, rather than immediately retaliating in word or actions, you talk to God. You might just hear Him saying, "That person doesn't know Me yet. Show them My grace and forgiveness." How would that change your response? Our interaction and our responses to people can be an instrument of God or an instrument of Satan. The biggest impact we can have for the kingdom can be in the responses to our own errors, offenses and sins. This is where a Godly perspective is absolutely imperative. When we react without God, out of our own human, fleshly and self-serving perspective, it will often leave others crushed and spiritually crippled as we walk away feeling validated. I have learned, with the Spirits help, to strive to live out this important truth. God wants us to have an "others first" perspective.

Philippians 2:3-4

Do nothing out of selfish ambition or vain conceit, but in humility consider others better than yourselves. Each of you should look not only to your own interests, but also to the interests of others.

This is the only conclusion we can possibly draw as we walk through the steps of the Ephesians 6 Battle Plan. Truth, righteousness, peace, faith, salvation and the Word of God; consistently and overwhelmingly points to selflessness. It is only when we take the self-serving road that we will soon find ourselves alone and unable to fend off the devils advances. Alone we will sooner or later succumb to his relentless pursuit of our mind and thoughts. Unless we return to our unit and begin to execute the Battle Plan again, we will be devoured AS prey.

Chapter Eleven

Armed and Dangerous
(What were you thinking? You're The Venus de Milo?)

For many years I worked as the Property Sergeant at the Massachusetts Treatment Center for the sexually dangerous. Every inmate in that facility had been convicted of a major sex related crime. These inmates committed crimes such as rape, child molestation, bestiality and necrophilia. If you can name an unthinkable crime, one of these inmates had probably committed it. Many of them had not just committed these types of crimes, but they had also murdered their victims. I mention this to give you a picture of what a Correction Officer deals with on a daily basis.

As bad as the environment was, within the walls of this prison there was a place that was set apart from the rest of the blocks. This place was rightly called the Segregation Unit. This was a smaller housing unit with two sections of six cells each. This unit was designed for those inmates who were the worst of the worst. They couldn't, or wouldn't conform to the rules and regulations of the institution, and were constantly the root of problems and illegal activity. Part of my job was to control the property of these segregated inmates. Because they were housed in this special unit, they were not afforded some of the privileges which the inmates in normal population were given. The property allowed in a segregation cell was limited to the following items: 2 books or magazines (religious or non-religious), 1 towel, 1 face cloth, 1 bar of soap, 2 T-shirts, 2 undershorts, 2 pair of socks, 2 shirts, 2 pants, 1 pair of shoes, and 1 cubic foot of legal and/or writing material. It was part of my job to make a daily journey to the Segregation Unit and collect each inmate's "Property Exchange Request Form" and process those requests according to the written procedures. It was not uncommon for me to arrive with a cart full of legal material for an inmate to look through in order to exchange some of the material he had for some new materials. Because the inmates were now housed in a limited property area, the Property Sergeant was responsible for all the property which had been confiscated from the inmate's original cell. Inevitably, during these visits, these inmates would request to have more legal material than the rules allowed for.

Remember the limit for the Segregation Unit is 1 cubic foot of legal material. I literally used a plastic milk crate to measure each inmate's material. If you were not aware, most plastic milk crates are exactly 1 cubic foot. One day, a particular inmate who was being housed in the Segregation Unit, insisted that he needed this additional pile of legal material. I handed him the Request Form and informed him that I would process his request as quickly as possible, but in the mean time, he would have to make his selection of one cubic foot of legal material.

At this time I would like to reveal a weakness in my character which most of the time I was easily able to control but occasionally, during my career, the stress level of working in the prison would kind of "sneak up" on me. I wasn't always openly aware when I was coming to a blow up point. Sometimes, to my surprise, a confrontation or a difficult circumstance would trigger an irrational and often dangerous response. This confrontation triggered one of these irrational responses.

The inmate became more and more irritated and began to refuse to relinquish his excessive legal material. During this exchange I was the only officer on the floor, and there were three inmates out of there cells for property exchange, exercise and legal calls. The inmate I was dealing with was not only refusing to give up his extra legal material, but he also began to taunt me by saying, "You think you're so tough because you wear a badge. If you didn't have that badge on, I would kick your butt!" Something in me had reached the breaking point and any hope of a controlled, reasonable response flew out my head.

I grabbed a hold of the badge which was pinned on my chest and yanked it off along with a patch of material from my shirt. I slammed it onto the metal table and walked directly up to the inmate, stopping when my nose literally touched his nose. I believe that he could see the fire in my eyes because his entire expression changed. I spoke softly but intensely as I said, "My badge is on the table and I'm standing right here. Are you gonna keep runnin' your mouth or are you all talk?" I have to admit, it wasn't one of my best decisions. What happened next even surprised me. The other two inmates came along side of the inmate, took his arms and while backing him up, implored him to knock it off saying, "Why are you giving Jeff a hard time? He's always been fair with us!"

Whenever I recall this event from my past I can't help but think of two things; first, how foolish I was for losing my composer (don't worry God has sanded that character flaw right down) and secondly, and more in line with the subject matter, the symbolism that comes with wearing a badge. The badge is, in reality, nothing but a piece of metal. It has no protective properties in and of itself. But in both of our minds, the inmate's as well as mine, it symbolized something; it symbolized authority, protection and boundaries. The truth was, even though I ripped that badge off my shirt, my authority never left. The only thing that was actually accomplished was that I ruined my shirt! Even though I no longer wore the badge, the boundaries still existed and the inmate was unwilling to cross them. Even though the badge was gone, its symbolic protection was still maintained.

The same thing can be said of the armor of God. The symbolic armor from Ephesians chapter six has great significance. Whether we understand it fully or not, this armor is effective and will make the enemy think twice before "runnin' his mouth."

I would like to take some time and explain the significance of the armor and show you just how much protection and authority we are afforded by this Battle Plan for resolving conflicts.

Ephesians 6:14-17

Stand firm then, with the belt of truth buckled around your waist, with the breastplate of righteousness in place, and with your feet fitted with the readiness that comes from the gospel of peace. In addition to all this, take up the shield of faith, with which you can extinguish all the flaming arrows of the evil one. Take the helmet of salvation and the sword of the Spirit, which is the word of God.

The "Belt of Truth" is the first piece of armor I will describe. The belt that was used in battle during the first century was not like the belt that we use today to hold up our pants. It was a belt that buckled in the back. The front was a piece of Armor that protected the core of the warrior. God connects this piece of armor to truth because truth has to be protected if we are going to have any hope of winning a battle. If the enemy can wound us in our core, if he can get us to believe lies, or others to believe lies about us, then he has struck a blow that will lead to destruction if it is not addressed. Is it any wonder that God not only links truth to this type of belt, but He lists it first to denote its grave importance? Without truth we are doomed to draw bad conclusions, take erroneous steps and walk farther and farther from a resolution or from reconciliation. The Belt of Truth protects our core. Because lies can be the catalyst of many conflicts, it is of first and great importance to guard the truth. Protect your core with the Belt of Truth and you will soon discover the road to reconciliation.

The next piece of armor is the "Breastplate of Righteousness." As we explained earlier, righteousness, in this context, is not perfection, it is choosing to do things God's way. The reason this is attached to a metaphorical breastplate is because righteousness is a heart condition.

If we willingly choose to seek and act in God directed ways, our heart will be protected. Biblical actions and attitudes will not only protect the heart, they will flow from the heart. I am constantly amazed at the impact this simple step in the Battle Plan has on the people we encounter in life.

Our feet are fitted with the readiness that comes from the Gospel of Peace. This, at first glance seems to be a little difficult to get a handle on (or in this case a footle). But for those of us who aren't particularly blessed by walking around barefoot, we can totally understand what is being conveyed here. I am one of those people who are just more comfortable with something on my feet. I would not feel at peace or ready for action without some type of footwear. I would feel vulnerable and somewhat exposed. Being without shoes, especially on rough terrain, causes me to feel uneasy and anxious. But when I have the proper footwear for whatever activity I am doing, I am totally at peace and I am ready to move. Our feet are our mode of transportation. In the first century, when soldiers were at war, if they incurred a foot injury they were virtually useless to the remainder of the platoon. They became a liability and were often left behind to fend for themselves as the army advanced. Having our feet secure and ready means that we have peace of mind and we know that we can answer the call and respond to defend ourselves or come to the defense of others under attack.

In addition we are called to take up the "Shield of Faith." I'm sure it isn't difficult for anyone to picture faith as a shield. These first century shields came in several sizes for various uses. First of all there was a small circular shield that was very useful in hand to hand combat. It slid onto the arm opposite the soldier's weapon bearing arm and could be easily wielded to defend a strike from an opposing soldier. There was also a very large shield that nearly covered the entire body of a soldier.

These shields were used to defend soldiers in groups or platoon formation. The front line of soldiers would march in close formation and hold these long shields in front of them as the army advanced. The soldiers behind could also hold these long shields above their heads to guard against arrows being fired in an arc over the front shields. The amazing thing about faith is its ability to strengthen and grow. So if our faith is small it is still very useful to ward off the attacks of a lone combatant. But we had better be prepared not to venture out too often from the protection of the platoon where our combined faith can protect us from attacks from multiple angles. Our faith is what protects us from the enemy and our combined faith with our brothers and sisters in the Body of Christ can protect us from attacks that we may have never seen coming.

Next we are to put on the "Helmet of Salvation." The head wound is potentially an instantaneously lethal wound. Having a helmet on is security against such a wound. Salvation in the sense of ones eternal destiny as well as in the sense of being rescued or delivered from circumstances is the picture we can glean from this symbolic helmet. When a soldier is battling without a helmet he is never quite secure because he knows that he is vulnerable from any and every angle. But having a helmet securely in place enables him to focus on the mission at hand. He won't be concerned about a stray arrow or glancing blow to the head because he knows his helmet will absorb the blow. Our secure status in the kingdom of God has that same effect on the believer. The Christian can feel safe in knowing that his eternal destiny is secure and any and all circumstances will work out to the Glory of God. The helmet of salvation ensures that his mind and thoughts are safe and secure from the enemy's attacks.

Finally, the only offensive piece of equipment in the entire list; the "Sword of The Spirit, which is the Word of God." Remember we discussed the Greek word used in this portion of scripture is (rhema) or spoken word. The use of the word (rhema) reveals to us that we have many, many swords to use against the enemy. Jesus modeled this for us when He was tempted in the desert. He answered Satan every time by quoting a different verse of scripture. Jesus used a different weapon for each separate attack because each attack was aimed differently. We must read and know the Word of God. Each truth from Scripture is a separate weapon against the many lies Satan and his minions will attempt to throw at us. The most effective weapon against any attack is to hit each lie with the opposing truth from Scripture. This is what Jesus modeled and this a lethal weapon against the enemy.

If you'll notice we are actually right back at truth again. But this time it is in the form of truth responses taken from the Bible. No soldier worth his salt would go into battle without a weapon, his sword, or as we have discovered, swords. Yet, how often do we enter into conflict without ever consulting what God's Word has to say about our circumstances? Too Often! Even once is too often. How can we expect to win a battle without any weapons? If we want to be victorious in these battles that arise in our lives, we had better take these armaments seriously. If we don't, our effectiveness for the kingdom will be greatly diminished. Our testimony will be tarnished and even worse, ministries will be dragged through the mud. The most devastating part about this is people do not see the damage they are doing to the church or to the Name of Jesus when they try to bulldoze their way through conflict and never even open the Scriptures that are able to equip us for every good work.

2 Timothy 3:16-17

All Scripture is God-breathed and is useful for teaching, rebuking, correcting and training in righteousness, so that the man of God may be thoroughly equipped for every good work.

As we put on the armor of God we are not just putting on a belt, a breastplate, a pair of shoes, a shield, a helmet and a sword. We are putting on Christ. Each of the steps of the Battle Plan is also used in Scripture as a description of Jesus. Truth (John 4:6), Righteousness (1 Cor. 1:30), Peace (Acts 10:36), Faith (Heb. 12:2), Salvation (Psalm 95:1), and of course The Word (John 1:1).

This armor, which we can put on each day, is symbolic of putting on Christ himself. Imagine the impact we would have on our community if we would speak, act and live wearing

Christ as our armor. There would be no conflict we would not see approaching, no temptation we could not turn from and no attacks from the enemy we could not withstand. Are we armed and ready or are we The Venus de Milo?

Chapter Twelve

May I Take Your Order?
(Not until I check the whole menu)

During my last few years in the Massachusetts Department of Correction I was a Lieutenant at the Bridgewater State Hospital for the criminally insane (doesn't that sound fun?). I had many duties and responsibilities depending on my assignment. One of my duties was to oversee the arrival of new inmates coming into the institution from court, jail or other prisons. This helped to ensure the transfer of custody from one law enforcement agency to another was done legally and without incident. On one occasion I was overseeing a transfer of custody from the Plymouth County Sherriff department to the State D.O.C. As I was observing a very young Sheriff, who had custody of the new arrival, he seemed very nervous as he began to remove the mechanical restraints from the inmate. This was a normal part of the process as hand-cuffs, waist chains and leg-irons do not stay with the inmate when his custody is transferred from one agency to another.

However, an officer should never begin to remove full restraints without another officer physically present in the room. Further more, there is a proper order to removing mechanical restraints, which ensures the security of the inmate as well as the safety of the officer. As the inmate sat on a bench within the transfer cell, the young Sherriff removed the inmate's hand cuffs and placed them on the bench next to the inmate. Not only were the inmate's hands now free, but also the officer was kneeling down directly in front of the inmate, and his head was looking down at the inmate's feet as he proceeded to begin removing the inmate's leg irons.

My duties require me to observe the transfer from outside the cell from either a video monitor or directly from the outer hallway. Since I had positioned myself in the hallway, I entered the cell as the potential risk to the officer was greater than my ability to stand by and watch. As the Sherriff was unlocking the inmates leg irons I entered the cell, picked up the hand cuffs from the bench and stood close to the Sherriff to ensure his safety. After the inmate's restraints had been removed and we both had exited the cell, I discretely took the Sherriff aside and explained to him the proper order, positioning and posture to use while unshackling an inmate.

First, and most importantly, an officer should wait for their partner to be present. This simple step will help eliminate ninety percent of all potential problems. Secondly the hand-cuffs should not have been removed first and should never, ever be placed within arms reach of the inmate. The Officer should position himself behind the inmate, removing the leg irons first and then the hand cuffs or waist chains last. Working from behind the inmate gives the Officer the best defensive position should the inmate become combative.

As I shared this process with the young Officer, I prefaced it by saying, "Let me share some things with you that just might save your life one day." With that opening phrase, I had his complete and undivided attention. He received the instructions with gratitude and I believe it made a profound difference in how he approached his job.

From this final story I would like to "...share something with you that might just save your life someday," spiritually speaking. The order of steps in this Battle Plan cannot be skipped or done halfway. In fact, some of them may need to be repeated. On my own journey, I have had to return to step number one many, many times. For this reason I am laying out each step in a shorter format in this chapter. I pray that this quick reference section might help many in conflict to first of all memorize the steps and the verses connected to them, and secondly to diligently work through each step in the process and return to them as needed. I cannot emphasize this enough, be sure to follow the biblical order, which has been given to us. Be prayerful and thorough as you work through each step. Be more than thorough, even if you believe you have completed a step, continue to pray for greater understanding and insight to your circumstances before moving onto the next step of the Battle Plan. Read the whole menu before ordering.

The Biblical Battle Plan:
Ephesians 6:13-17 (bold mine)

Therefore put on the full armor of God, so that when the day of evil comes, you may be able to stand your ground, and after you have done everything, to stand. Stand firm then, with the belt of ***truth*** *buckled around your waist, with the breastplate of* ***righteousness*** *in place, and with your feet fitted with the readiness that comes from the gospel of* ***peace****. In addition to all this, take up the shield of* ***faith****, with which you can extinguish all the flaming arrows of the evil one. Take the helmet of* ***salvation*** *and the sword of the Spirit, which is the* ***word of God****.*

The Battle Plan—Step # 1—Truth

Remember Truth is a belt, which protects the core. It is the foundational step to the entire Battle Plan. You will most likely need to return to this step many times throughout the battle. But it will be well worth it. Every time you return to Truth it opens the pathway to continue in the battle. If you believe even one lie on your journey, it has the potential to render the Battle Plan ineffective while at the same time diminishing the hopes of reconciliation.

Truth Actions:

Pray
How you pray gives God a chance to move. Pray for the source of your conflict

- Pray for the person (people) with whom you are having conflict.
- DO NOT pray for them to see it your way.
- Pray that the Lord would help you understand their perspective, and their view of you.
- Pray that God would help you begin this process to find truth, not to justify your case.
- Pray for God to help you bring glory to Him through this conflict and process.

Capture
Taking control of your thoughts before they get away from you is of vital importance.
"Take every thought captive and make it obedient to Christ?" (2 Cor. 10:5)

- What does Jesus think of your thoughts? What does His Word say about them?
- Separate what you KNOW to be true from what you THINK might be true.
- Pray and confess the things you have been holding on to that are not truth.

Investigate

Gathering ALL the information you believe will keep you focused on truth.

- Pray the Holy Spirit will reveal to you more helpful information.
- Seek out impartial, mature Christian friends for an honest assessment of your situation.
- Sort out what you know about the conflict, those involved, and what may be going on in their lives that might help you get a better perspective.

Note: If you have only one perspective (yours) you **DO NOT** have **ALL** the information.

Self-assess

Once you feel you have as much information as possible, answer the following questions:

- Do you feel humbled by the discovery of the truth, knowing it didn't support you?
- Do you feel a sense of pride by the discovery of truth, knowing it supported you?

Confess

Discovering truth confirms the Holy Spirit is working. Righteousness comes when we confirm His work, and align ourselves with what He desires from us.

- Confess where pride has crept in, and ask God to help you gain His heart in this matter. Pride is a feeling that does not line up with Scripture (Phil 2:3-4).
- Confirm where God has humbled you, and thank Him for aligning you with truth. Ask Him to help you respond from this point with total humility to all those involved.

Now that you have taken a prayerful look at yourself and your conflict in the light of truth, look up in your Bible these verses connected to truth. Write down any thoughts or other verses that God brings to your mind in the Truth Notes section.

Truth Verses: John 8:44; John 14:6; Romans 12:3; 2 Corinthians 10:5

Truth Notes:

The Battle Plan—Step # 2—Righteousness

Righteousness is a breastplate protecting the heart. Obedience to God and His Word is a heart condition. The meaning of righteousness in this context is to do things God's way. Our second step is discovering what the Bible says about our circumstance: our situation; our response; our attitude and our action?

Righteousness Actions:

Identify

Being able to identify the topic or area of conflict can help you toward a solution.

- Identify your circumstances as a general concept.
- Lies, finances, relationships, slander, offended, communication, work, etc.
- Find and study the portions of Scripture pertaining to your situation.
- If you are not used to navigating the Bible for answers ask someone for help.
- List those verses/passages that speak to your issue.

Listen

What are these verses telling you about your responses and attitudes?

- Have you been responding in a righteous way?
- What steps can you take to line your actions up with the Bible?

Pray

God may have led you to the proper actions, but what about the when's, how's and what's?

- Pray about God's timing for addressing the conflict.
- Pray about who should be present when you address the other person (people).
- Pray for God to reveal any other truth you are not seeing.
- Pray about your reaction to ALL possible responses by the other person (people).

Write

I suggest taking the time to write your action steps down to form a Righteous Action Plan.

- Write your plan down to help you evaluate its benefits and problems.
- Pray about your plan, and adjust or add to it as The Spirit leads.

Consult

After considering your approach to your conflict, consider all possible responses.

- Ask a trusted friend to walk with you through your approach.
- Be open to loving, constructive, biblical suggestions.
- How am I expecting the other person (people) to react?
- Is there a different approach that might help alleviate negative reactions?
- How will I handle a negative reaction to my righteous response?

Righteousness Verses: Genesis 15:6; Luke 17:3; 2 Timothy 3:16-17; Titus 3:5

Righteousness Notes:

The Battle Plan—Step # 3—Peace

Your feet are fitted with the Gospel of Peace. Your Righteous Action Plan is completed and ready to be implemented. You are ready to move. That is why Peace is in the form of footwear. Remember this is "good news" the gospel of peace. You have received peace through righteousness and now you will bring peace to those whom you are in conflict with.

Peace Actions:

Identify

Take the time to go to a quiet place and identify if your heart is still in conflict or at peace.

- A person in conflict will often have thoughts of comebacks and retaliation.
- A person in conflict has difficulty thinking of anything but the conflict.
- A person at peace is comfortable with themselves as well as the others involved.
- A person at peace knows they have done all that the Bible has directed them to do.
- A person at peace is open to and even desiring reconciliation.

Prepare

Has your righteous action plan been completed and do you feel a measure of peace in your heart?

- If you do not feel peace about your action plan, continue praying for direction.
- Do not let this peace leave you unprepared for a potential negative response.

- Even though you may now be responding biblically, the other person involved may not.
- Will you still walk and respond in peace if you receive a negative response?

Self-Test

Have the negative thoughts that were racing through your mind decreased or even stopped?

- If you have followed the first two steps you should be sensing a decrease in spiritual attacks. Is this true for you?
- When you bathe yourself in truth, and act in righteousness, Satan WILL flee.
- The resulting void of the presence of evil and lies should be Peace.
- Begin to embrace this peace, even if it is small in scope and time.
- Peace, even in small doses, is often confirmation of proper perspective and direction.
- Continued and increasing peace is a catalyst for a changed life.

Warning

Are you experiencing a false sense of peace?

- Be warned! True peace can only be found in righteous actions.
- Actions that line up with the Word of God bring TRUE peace.
- Actions that go against a biblical directive CANNOT bring true peace.
- False peace will be Satan temporarily ceasing his attacks in support of your NON-BIBLICAL actions.

- You may believe you have made the correct decision…
- But how does it compare to Scripture?
- Remember true peace is realized not just through your thoughts and actions—but are verified as they align with biblical truths.

Peace Verses: Psalm 119:105; John 16:33; Romans 5:1; James 4:5-7

Note: If you have devised a righteous action plan and acted on it, you should experience some sense of peace immediately. The Battle Plan's steps of Truth and Righteousness will lead you to Peace. If you have not felt any peace you may need to return to Truth and begin again. The peace you receive will also be the peace you bring to those involved in the conflict. Remember battle wounds sometimes take time to heal. Continue to be the catalyst for peace and reconciliation.

Peace Notes:

The Battle Plan—Step # 4—Faith

Faith is a shield. It is the protection we have from the enemy's attacks. The greatest part about this shield is that it doesn't have to stay the same size. Our shield can grow larger and protect us better. God's Word and the power of His Truth, Righteousness and Peace will grow our Faith. Our growing faith will in turn protect us better and can also protect others we are close to if we share our faith journey.

Faith Actions:

Assess

As you have trusted God and His Word for your righteous response to your conflict, have you felt your faith in God strengthen?

- Do you feel more confident in God's Word?
- Do you feel a closer connection to the Holy Spirit within you?

Share

Do you have a person, small group or fellowship where you can share your journey?

- Your journey may help someone else through a conflict they are going through.
- You may even get a greater perspective from others who have had a similar experience.

Alert

Are you watching for increased attacks from the enemy?

- Are you taking every thought captive?

- Are you continuing to weigh them against the truth of God's Word?
- Do you have a group or a mentor where you can safely process thoughts?

Faith Verses: John 16:33; 2 Corinthians 12:10; Hebrews 11:1; Philippians 1:6

Faith Notes:

The Battle Plan—Step # 5—Salvation

The Helmet of Salvation as you may recall protects the head and brings an assurance of being delivered, rescued or being safe from any and all attacks that might render a soldier incapacitated and potentially killed in the battle.

Salvation Actions:

Salvation

Do you understand the difference between eternal, spiritual salvation and circumstantial, physical salvation?
Have you experienced eternal, spiritual salvation?

- If not, you can pray and seek God's forgiveness right now. (return to chapter 3 for salvation plan)
- Are you part of a church fellowship or small group where you can ask for help in this area?
- Ask your pastor or small group leader to show you through God's Word how you can experience this eternal salvation.

Results

Do you feel like you have been saved or rescued from your conflict?

- Have you put each step into action and achieved the desired result?
- If not, what area(s) continue to trouble you?
- Are you still experiencing conflict?
- Have you proceeded through the Battle Plan alone?
- I would highly suggest inviting someone into the battle to help.

Responsibilities

If the other party to the conflict has not responded well—what is your responsibility?

- Have you done each step fully and sincerely?
- Have you experienced peace and increased faith?
- If you can answer yes to these questions then you have done all you can do.

Release

How can I feel peace and salvation if the other person is still in conflict with me?

- Are you still in conflict with them?
- If you answered yes—then you need to return to The Battle Plan.
- If you are still feeling conflict you missed something between Truth and Peace.
- If you answered no—then you have properly executed the Battle Plan.
- Remember you can only control your actions, attitudes and responses.

Pray

Continue to pray for the other person in your conflict.

- Pray that they might experience the same peace you have discovered.
- Look for opportunities to bless them (Romans 12:14-21).
- **Do Not** let their actions or attitudes change your new perspective of them.

Salvation Verses: (Romans 10:8-10 Eternal, Spiritual Salvation); Psalm 96:27; James 4:6-7

Salvation Notes:

The Battle Plan—Step # 6—The Word of God

The Word of God is described as the Sword of the Spirit. The only offensive weapons we have. We need to pick it up, learn and train with it so that we know when and how to use it properly. When the devil begins to attack us with lies, we must learn to counter his attacks with apposing, biblical truth. Even if we just begin by reading the Bible daily we will soon find ourselves better prepared to identify conflict as it arises, or better yet before it draws us into a battle.

Word of God Actions:

Support

Are you currently attending a Bible believing Church?

- Does your church teach from the Bible?
- Does your church have Bible studies or small groups for further learning and study?
- Is the Bible said to be the only source for truth by your church leaders?
- Do you feel alone in your battle with conflict and life's circumstances?
- God never intended for us to do life alone—The church is His presence in our life.
- The Church is called "The Body of Christ"
- The body is made up of many parts that support each other.
- Somewhere there is a Body that needs you and will embrace you.

Confirm

Are you currently involved in a Bible study or small group?

- Do you participate in the group with questions or comments?
- Are your questions being answered to your satisfaction in this group?
- Are the answers to your questions agreeing with what the Bible says?

Pray

If you are **not** currently attending a Bible believing church please pray about your situation.

- If your church does not use the Bible, pray about looking elsewhere for spiritual truth.
- If you are not attending any church at all please pray about seeking out a fellowship.

Word

Have you been using your Bible as you executed The Battle Plan?

- It's important to know where the verses are in Scripture and not just know about them.
- Have you discovered any verses that might help you avoid a similar conflict in the future?

Write

Take the time to write about your experience of working through the Battle Plan.

- Search the Bible for more weapons for future battles.
- Discover through Scripture how to avoid this type of conflict in the future.
- Try to journal or blog your journey in Truth.

Word of God Verses: Eph. 4:11-14; Heb. 10:23-25; 2 Tim. 3:16-17; 1 Peter 5:8; 2 Peter 2:1;
Jude 19

Word of God Notes:

Conclusion

As I come to the final chapter it is important to understand the reality of this Battle Plan. Even though we might have taken the steps necessary to work toward reconciliation, the process in most cases is a continuing one. What I mean is this; just because everything is now out in the open, and perhaps forgiveness has been asked for and received, things don't always return to the way they were. Conflict, even resolved conflict, has a way of leaving people with feelings of mistrust, uneasiness or a guarded approach to interaction. These are natural, unintended by-products of conflict. The longer the wait to address an issue, the greater the residual effects will be. In my own case I believe that those who were offended had a real sense of relief knowing that I was now aware of how I had affected our relationship, and steps were being made to improve our interaction. However, in my own heart and mind I became very tentative and unsure of myself in the area of offering opinions and ideas. This was directly related to the length of time it had taken for my offenses to be brought to my attention. Some of my hesitation was, admittedly another attack of the enemy. I would hear the enemy in my thoughts, "You can't stop offending people. You should just quit, pack it up, you shouldn't be a Pastor!"

These were lies being whispered in my minds ear. Again and again I would take these thoughts captive and make them obedient to Christ and His calling on my life. Even as I was continually striving to live in truth, there was a real sense of wondering if I would unintentionally say or do something offensive again. Would the same people be willing to bring it to my attention quickly or would they silently harbor bad feelings toward me? Using the Sword of The Spirit to respond to those spiritual attacks with opposing, Biblical truth was the key element to moving forward in ministry. These residual feelings subsided and healthy dialogue soon replaced tentative conversation. The catalyst for us was open and honest conversations.

Speak the truth in love, and the potential for an even closer relationship with a foundation of safety with one another will begin to grow. Your confidence will grow, as your new relationship becomes one that can say and receive the hard stuff knowing it's for love and the kingdom of God and no other reasons.

There is another aspect to this process that must be understood. It may seem obvious but it is often overlooked. All people are created differently! We are all wired to act and react in ways that are uniquely us. Some people are able to address conflict without hesitation and others will avoid conflict at all costs. Most people are somewhere in the middle. Those of us who are on the extreme edges have to walk this path with much prayer and counsel. There are pitfalls for the extremes. Though they are different, they can be equally destructive. Let me explain: people who have no problem addressing conflict, will see an issue and head directly toward a resolution. The down side to this approach; what if the other people involved are not ready to address the issue? Not ready emotionally, not ready spiritually, and certainly not ready for a meeting filled with tension. Coming together to work things out may be absolutely the correct approach. But if it's put into practice at the wrong time, the process can be seriously hindered rather than resolved. On the other hand, people who avoid conflict inevitably spend large amounts of time harboring bad feelings, anger and an overall sense of growing uneasiness. All the while the offender may, unknowingly continue to offend which only expands the gulf between them. Both of these extremes can damage relationships and slow, or even trample, any hope of reconciliation.

For these personalities, as well as every variation in between, the battle must be approached by laying a foundation of prayer prior to and during your entering into step number one. Prayer and truth is the only foundation strong enough to support the weight of this Biblical Battle Plan. Without truth the structure will inevitably collapse and without prayer the relationship will be irreparably harmed. Satan will be lying to you continuously. His desire is for conflict and un-forgiveness to be embedded into our hearts. The devil's intended results are division and continuing conflict.

It is my prayer that the Battle Plan in this book will reveal Satan's part in whatever conflict you find yourself. Resist him and his attack of lies and deceit, and he will flee. Truth and lies cannot occupy the same space. Don't let him devour you in his wave of destruction. As the devil flees you can now approach your conflict with a heart prepared for forgiveness and reconciliation. Trust me when I write; it isn't always best to be right. Even when we are in the right, if we are not walking in humility and prepared to forgive others, we will seldom experience the peace that comes from a righteous life. The words of the prophet Micah must be the desire of our heart.

Micah 6:8

And what does the LORD require of you? To act justly and to love mercy and to walk humbly with your God.

My prayer is for you to gain a deeper and more intimate understanding of the core principle at work throughout this battle plan—the principle of forgiveness. When our hearts are bent toward forgiveness then we are truly Christ's ambassadors. We should be prepared to forgive those who have offended us as well as quick to ask forgiveness of anyone whom we have intentionally or unintentionally offended.

Let me be clear about this one thing, this does not mean that we are to become a target for anyone who wants to take advantage of us. We are not instructed to take abuse. But we are certainly called as believers to be the personification of forgiveness. The world will never understand the forgiveness offered to them by the Creator if they never see that same forgiveness lived out by those of us who are in the best position to model it; those who have called on the name of the Lord Jesus as Savior. We have been given the very words of life. We have been called to read, know and live out the principles of righteousness from God's Word. How can we expect a hurting world to turn to Jesus when we are not even willing to change how we act and react in times of conflict? I leave you with the verse that was my guide through this process and I have returned to time and time again ever since.

2 Corinthians 10:5

We demolish arguments and every pretension that sets itself up against the knowledge of God, and we take captive every thought to make it obedient to Christ.

Guard your thoughts and your mind. It is the portal the enemy will use to draw you into conflict. I have come to a point in my walk with God where I purposefully think the best of those who might offend me. I choose to believe their words or actions were not meant to offend. I am intentionally assuming the best of people. If offensive words or actions continue, I will go directly to the person and simply explain my understanding of what was said or done, express the offense which could be perceived, and simply ask if I heard or received the message correctly. This practice has yielded many apologies, and relationships which continue to grow closer because of the honesty. This practice has also revealed some harbored feelings of anger and resentment. But it also opened the door for some meaningful and restorative conversation. If offenses and bad feelings are left unspoken and in the dark, Satan will inevitably begin his evil process of compounding and adding to any misinformation which may be sprinkled within the relationship. The devil prowls around like a roaring lion seeking Someone to Devour. Believe the best of people and put on the armor of God. We can win the spiritual battle within human conflict. God has shown us the devils battle plan but He has also given us His Battle Plan for defeating Satan and resolving conflict in our lives. Be fully prepared for the battle with; Truth, Righteousness, Peace, Faith, Salvation and The Word of God.

Endnotes

1 All Good People Go to Heaven?—*Jeff Barksdale, Publish America, www.jtbarksdale.com*

2 Bombings of Switzerland in World War II—Wikipedia, www.en.wikipedia.org

Some or all inmate quotes have been softened to accommodate all readers

All Bible quotes are taken from the New International Version.

CPSIA information can be obtained at www.ICGtesting.com
Printed in the USA
LVOW061736140112

263814LV00001BB/7/P

9 781462 633722